WHEN THE SMOKE CLEARS

WHEN THE SMOKE CLEARS

RICK WALL

WITH CAMERON CAINE OAM

Copyright © Rick Wall and Cameron Caine OAM

Published by Hembury Books in 2025

hemburybooks.com.au

info@hemburybooks.com

ISBN 9781764055284 (paperback)

ISBN 9781764055277 (ebook)

The moral right of the author has been asserted.

All rights reserved. No portion of this book may be reproduced in any form without permission from the author and publisher, except as permitted by Australian copyright law.

 A catalogue record for this book is available from the National Library of Australia

Dedicated to the Caine and Buchanan families – past, present and future

Some of the material in this book may be distressing to survivors of the 2009 bushfires, their family and friends, as well as members of the general public. If you need support, please contact Lifeline on 13 11 14 or Beyond Blue on 1300 22 4636.

About the Authors

Journalist Rick Wall spent three decades in the media industry, most notably with Melbourne radio stations and as a researcher for ABC TV current affairs in Sydney.

When Black Saturday unfolded in 2009, Rick was semi-retired. Then, AFL Victoria decided to send someone to Kinglake to help rebuild the township's football and netball club. Rick was that person. He grew close to many of the locals who offered unique insights into the tragedy and the recovery. Rick donated his services to write the stories of the Caine and Buchanan families during the disaster and its painstaking aftermath.

Cameron Caine OAM grew up in northeast Melbourne. After a 15-year career as a plumber, in 1999 he joined Victoria Police and served in various stations, including Reservoir and Seymour, before transferring to Kinglake, where he was one of only two local police officers on duty on Black Saturday. He retired in 2019 due to PTSD.

Throughout his career, he was honoured with several awards, including the Medal of the Order of Australia (OAM), the Victoria Police Valour Award, the Royal Humane Society of Australasia Silver Medal for Bravery, the Commendation for Brave Conduct, and the National Medal for Service. He is still involved with the Kinglake Football Netball Club and continues to contribute to his community through creative projects.

Foreword by Shane Warne

When I was asked if I could write the foreword for this book I was extremely honoured. This isn't just a story about tragedy, it's a story about the strength of the human spirit and a sense of community through what could only be described as one of the most frightening and horrific moments in Australian history. It's a moment in time that touched every Australian and many other people around the world.

I remember, as do most of us, exactly where I was when I heard about the fires. Melbourne had a heatwave that week and I was home with the kids in the pool; there was a haze over Melbourne that was eerie. It turned out to be the smoke from the fires (over an hour's drive away). The temperature was well over 40 degrees and had been for five consecutive days. We all sat watching the news updates and just couldn't believe what was happening, I think every Australian who was watching the TV could not believe what they were witnessing.

I felt I had to do something, although I was not sure what or how. A group of us got together with a bunch of sporting equipment and drove to Kinglake to help in some way. Families were already dealing with more than any of us could ever understand, it was a matter of just being there and lending support by way of a shoulder to cry on or an emotional ear. It's difficult to describe the emotion that we were experiencing; it really was one of shock. This was the first of many trips I made to the fire-stricken areas. It is here that I first met Aiden Buchanan and his family.

Aiden wasn't much older than my son, Jackson. He had lost two siblings in the fires, his brother Macca and his sister Neeve. I remember clearly Aiden had a beanie on, and I said, "I like your beanie mate," and he said, "It's my brother's." He cried, for what I was told was the first time since that devastating day. We connected straight away. I made a pact with him that I would continue to help Aiden and his family, and I have to this day. It's a special bond we have and one that I cherish. In such horrific times it's always down the track when everyone is trying to move on with their lives that these families need the most support.

When things settled down a bit and Coldplay were touring my good friend Chris Martin wanted to help too. So we both went up to meet Aiden and his friends at school, along with other affected schools, to try and put a smile on the children's faces. Chris was fantastic.

Then the Shane Warne Foundation and Variety, the children's charity, wasted no time teaming up to raise funds for the children impacted by what is now known as Black Saturday. The Shane Warne Foundation kicked off the fund with a $100,000 donation. As both organisations are focused on improving the lives of children the funds were welcomed by the large numbers who were recovering from the devastation.

The families which have suffered such tragic losses have had to find strength that I'm sure they never thought they had. However, through adversity, friendships were born and above all the human compassion and spirit is alive and well. The other good news is that people out there are still supporting the children, schools and families to this day. Long may it continue.

Shane Warne 2012

Shane Warne is an Australian sporting legend and one of the greatest cricketers to ever grace the international playing fields. Tragically, he died of heart failure in 2022.

Shane Warne with Aiden Buchanan, February 2009. (Pic: family collection.)

CONTENTS

Introduction xvii

PART ONE | 1

Chapter 1: Someone Else's Problem 3
Chapter 2: A Fire Tsunami 17
Chapter 3: On the Run 29
Chapter 4: The Fight of Their Lives 37
Chapter 5: Catastrophe 47
Chapter 6: Into the Chaos 55
Chapter 7: A Night of Mayhem 67
Chapter 8: My Town is Gone 83
Chapter 9: The Freight Trains Cometh 93
Chapter 10: Ross Tackles the Media 97
Chapter 11: Coping 109
Chapter 12: Not Coping 119
Chapter 13: New Goals 127
Chapter 14: Rising from the Ashes? .137
Chapter 15: The Hardest Thing 149
Chapter 16: More Money Matters 159
Chapter 17: The Slippery Slope 167
Chapter 18: Some Much-Needed Traction 175

PART TWO | 181

Chapter 1: A Stroll in the Garden. 183
Chapter 2: Moving On?. 189
Chapter 3: Turning Back Time. 201
Chapter 4: Ross and Bec Say "Thank You". 207
Chapter 5: The Campaign Trail 223
Chapter 6: Finale 249
Ross and Cameron: Raw Thoughts. 255
Have We Learned?. 260
Notes to the General Public. 262
Notes to Victorian Disaster Relief Organisers. 264
Note to the Victims 267

Introduction

A timeline for the township of Kinglake, and the nearby communities of Pheasant Creek and Kinglake West, can be divided into events prior to February 7, 2009, and life in the aftermath of the Black Saturday disaster.

Before the conflagration Cameron Caine and Ross Buchanan had a nodding acquaintance which occasionally brought them together over a drink or two at the local football club. But on that fateful date a horrific set of circumstances changed their lives forever.

On the night of the tragic events, which claimed 173 lives, Cameron and Ross were at the Kinglake West Country Fire Authority (CFA) building as news of the Buchanan family losses raced through the community. It was to Cameron and Laura Caine that Ross turned during the darkest hours of his life.

Cameron was one of only two police officers to work through the night of chaos as Ross, and thousands of others, fled their Kinglake Ranges homes.

Following the fires both men emerged as community leaders. Cameron led the football and netball club as it helped rally the Kinglake Ranges community; he then became embroiled in a federal election and fought for the right to represent Kinglake people in Canberra.

Incredibly, Cameron's electoral fate had a direct bearing on the outcome of the 2010 Australian election that returned the Gillard Labor Government by a knife edge margin.

Ross slowly and painfully came to terms with his grief and emerged as a driving force behind the resurgence of the local music community. He played a key role as Kinglake musicians headlined a Melbourne concert and later performed a play which Ross had written and scored.

Essentially, Ross helped many Kinglakers feel good about themselves again.

PART ONE

CHAPTER 1

SOMEONE ELSE'S PROBLEM

Cameron Caine stood in soft powdery grey ash that was so deep it nearly spilled over the top of his police boots.

He could still feel the heat of the ash through the leather.

The Kinglake senior constable had gone with local Country Fire Authority (CFA) captain Paul Hendrie to look for friends in Ward Street, to the west of the Kinglake village. Although the sun was up it was still eerily dark with the ash floating through the air like a winter mist as it coated everything in a ghostly off-white.

A once vibrant local street was now chillingly quiet. No dogs barked. There were no sounds of traffic. No insects, no birds. No children. Everything was gone. The houses, the sheds, the people. Objects in the distance faded to a dull monochrome.

Cameron and Paul were too bewildered to speak. They knew implicitly their words would fall well short of describing what they were seeing.

It was 7 a.m. on February 8, 2009. About thirteen hours since fires had ripped through the unsuspecting Kinglake Ranges communities, and about thirteen and a half hours since Cameron had left for work and gazed at a stunning sunset filtering through the trees of the Kinglake National Park.

It was only when that "sunset" began to flicker and move that he realised the fire was on Kinglake's doorstep, unannounced.

Turn the clock forward seven months and Cameron is standing alongside Australian Prime Minister Kevin Rudd on the Woori Yallock football oval in the Yarra Valley to the east of Melbourne. It's the local grand final day. Cheer squad members from the Melbourne Demons, an Australian Football League club in the city, have come along to help, and in blustery conditions hold on tightly to the remnants of the green and gold banner they'd made especially for the Kinglake team.

Kevin, Cameron and five thousand others are waiting for Ross Buchanan to stride out onto the ground and lead them in a rendition of the national anthem.

But the organisers are getting edgy. Ross is missing.

Cameron and Ross had both been to hell, and Ross hadn't come back.

Cameron Caine is a big burly goateed footballer from Pheasant Creek, only a few kilometres from Kinglake, which sits atop one of the southernmost slopes of Australia's Great Dividing Range fifty-five kilometres north-east of Melbourne. He became president of the local football and netball club when it was going through tough times and about to close its doors.

In contrast, Ross Buchanan is diminutive and wiry with shaggy black hair and expressive hazel eyes which often seem to speak before he begins talking.

The two men knew each other well, Ross was a long time club sponsor, but they were never close mates. On the night of February 7, 2009, all that changed as their lives became forever intertwined. More than once they would cry in each other's arms.

Ross was one of a small minority of Victorians who were hard at work on the morning of the day we came to know as Black Saturday. People were bracing themselves for unprecedented sweltering temperatures and wild, energy sapping winds. They were staying indoors.

Melbournians regard temperatures in the high 30s as heatwave conditions but on this particular Saturday the weather bureau had predicted the mercury would hit the mid-40s.

Up until that summer it had been simply unthinkable for Melbourne to swelter day in and day out through temperatures so extreme they buckled rail lines. But in late January records were broken when it hit 43 degrees, 109 on the old Fahrenheit scale, on three consecutive days.

In weather terms these were unique times. Politicians and emergency services bosses warned that the State of Victoria faced its worst fire risk on record. By midmorning on February 7 hot dry northerly winds, which sucked the moisture out of everything they touched, were gusting between 80 and 100 kilometres an hour.

But Ross had some jobs to do. He had to keep his water pump installation and repair company ticking over. It was his family's meal ticket and he would do whatever was required to provide for wife Bec and their four children, Calum aged 17, Mackenzie (Macca) 15, Aiden 13 and the family's little princess, Neeve, 9.

Friends sometimes wrongly assumed the Buchanans were well off because they had their own business; Ross would always tell them that indeed he was rich, or as he put it, "rich in life, with a beautiful wife and four children".

Ross had met Rebecca when she was just 17 years old and studying at the Melbourne Textile College. His love for her was one of the few constants in his life. Before he could afford a car he had wooed her by bus, catching it from Thornbury in the northern suburbs all the way out to Research twenty kilometres away on the edge of Melbourne's sprawling suburbs.

In his quieter moments he would sometimes think that he got the better part of the deal.

Bec had piercing blue eyes that could look deeply into him and right through to the other side when she was angry. Her face seemed as if it had been designed to smile easily and languidly. Sometimes he saw his wife in the face of his daughter Neeve.

Bec had left early that Saturday morning for the Whittlesea Country Music Festival, twenty minutes away at the foot of the mountain. She was vice-president of the organising committee, and with one thousand music fans at the campsite there was no shortage of items on the checklist to tick off.

Ross took Calum to work at the local hardware store and petrol station just before 9 A.M. The teenager was about to begin an accounting course at university and was earning some pocket money by working his mother's normal shift.

Calum was only weeks away from his 18th birthday and was saving hard for a car.

He and Ross drove past a group of cyclists on the main Kinglake-Whittlesea road and joked how crazy the pedal pumpers were to be riding on a heatwave day. Ross also thought how sad the trees looked, as if they'd surrendered to the unrelenting sun and were willing to give up their leaves early, a month before autumn.

After dropping Calum off Ross had house calls to make at three properties. There was hardly anyone else on the roads, it seemed only he and the mad cyclists were out in the morning heat.

By 10 A.M. the mercury was already in the mid-30s, well beyond the comfort zone of most Melbournians and at midday the state was in meltdown mode as it hit 40 degrees.

Returning to his home on National Park Road at 12.30, Ross could see smoke way in the distance to the northwest and opened up the CFA's website for more details.

Forty minutes earlier power lines had come down at Kilmore East and fire had taken hold in a nearby pine plantation. The blaze had then been pushed towards the township of Wandong by the nor-westerlies.

It was about sixty kilometres away by road from Kinglake West to where the fire started but only half that distance if a straight line is drawn across the mountains. Australians tend to think of distances in terms of travel times, so psychologically Kilmore East was far away.

Even so Ross took some precautions and moved the remains of his winter firewood pile to the rear of the property, as far as possible from the house. He also took his pump stock from a shed that backed onto the national park and placed them in the middle of the backyard.

Ross kept regular watch on the CFA website and the wind cock in his backyard, which would give him a head start if he needed to plot the fire's behaviour. He was also hoping his community fireguard representative would call with information, as had been the case during the last big fires.

Fireguard members were employed by the CFA to advise locals about fire risks in their areas and to help set up networks of people who would phone around if an emergency was imminent.

When everything was done Ross called a CFA mate, Rod, who'd already been sent with the Kinglake West crew to fight the Kilmore East fire. Rod told him it was causing some problems at Wandong and Ross asked for updates if time allowed. In the ensuing chaos Rod didn't get a chance to call back and when eventually he was able to return home to his own brick house, just three doors down National Park Road from the Buchanans, it was burnt to the ground.

Ross had a good understanding of bushfires. The Buchanans had lived in the heavily timbered Kinglake ridge area for sixteen years and were as accustomed to the annual fire threat as they were to the Yuletide. They accepted it as the price they paid for their bucolic lifestyle.

A few years earlier, in 2006, a slow-moving bushfire caused by lightning nibbled at the edges of the Kinglake Ridge for three nail biting days before a weather change finally put it out.

In the back of his mind Ross completed a family roll call. Bec was safe in Whittlesea, one son was at work and the other two were home with him. Daughter Neeve had been dropped off with grandparents Mick and Jenny Clark at Kinglake village. With her blonde hair, blue eyes and impish grin Neeve was always a more than welcome guest at the Clark household.

There was also something a bit special about the Buchanans' youngest child. All parents like to think that about their children but in Neeve's case it was true. She would always add that extra dollop of excitement to kids' parties, and at the footy club adults found it easy to smile when she was around. She may have only been in grade four at school, but Neeve already had that elusive X factor.

Perhaps it's something they inherited. More likely it's the way the kids were raised because Macca, like Neeve, had a reputation for being the life of the party.

The teenager was the sort of boy others just wanted to hang with. He was a talented musician, pounding away on the drums at times, which was not always conducive to family harmony. Macca was also sporty, playing footy for local teams, skating and swimming.

Youngest son Aiden had a cheeky grin and the visage to light up a fashion shoot. He could also be a quiet observer.

Of growing importance to both boys, Macca and Aiden were very popular with girls, who seemed drawn to their gentle side and the blond-haired good looks they had inherited from Bec.

While Neeve stayed with Nan and Pop, her brothers Aiden and Macca tried to hide from the heat inside the family's house in Kinglake West. Of course, that meant Ross was going to compete with the boys for control of the internet throughout the afternoon! He needed to keep the CFA site open, even though they were in no immediate danger. The boys had other internet priorities.

In Whittlesea Bec and the music festival organising committee met just after midday to discuss a fire which they'd heard had started way over near Kilmore. They decided they'd get together again at 3 P.M. and re-assess the situation. But barely sixty minutes later they held an emergency meeting. The fire was on its way and it was heading in their direction. The campers were told to stay put.

At home in Pheasant Creek, Cameron Caine struggled with his new split-system air conditioner. While the family sweltered he fiddled with the remote control, trying to coax the machine into giving up some cold air. Frustratingly, it kept blowing hot air into the house on what was shaping up as the warmest day in the state's history.

As his own temperature started to rise Cam called a local tradie for help, then he and wife Laura bundled their young sons Harry and Angus into the car and headed for his parents' place about four kilometres away at Kinglake West. Cameron's folks were interstate at Byron Bay visiting his sister, but he knew their aircon unit would give his family some respite from the blast furnace weather. Their 19-year-old daughter Sian was already out and about with friends.

It was about 12.30 p.m.

From the Bushfires Royal Commission

11.49 a.m. – First calls come through of a fire at Saunders Road in Kilmore East, in a direct line only about thirty kilometres north-west of Kinglake West.

Kilmore Country Fire Authority volunteers and trucks were on their way within five minutes, however the CFA Kilmore Incident Control Centre (ICC), which would manage the fire fight, wasn't adequately staffed.

Coordinators at the Emergency Control Headquarters in Melbourne were unaware of this staffing issue.

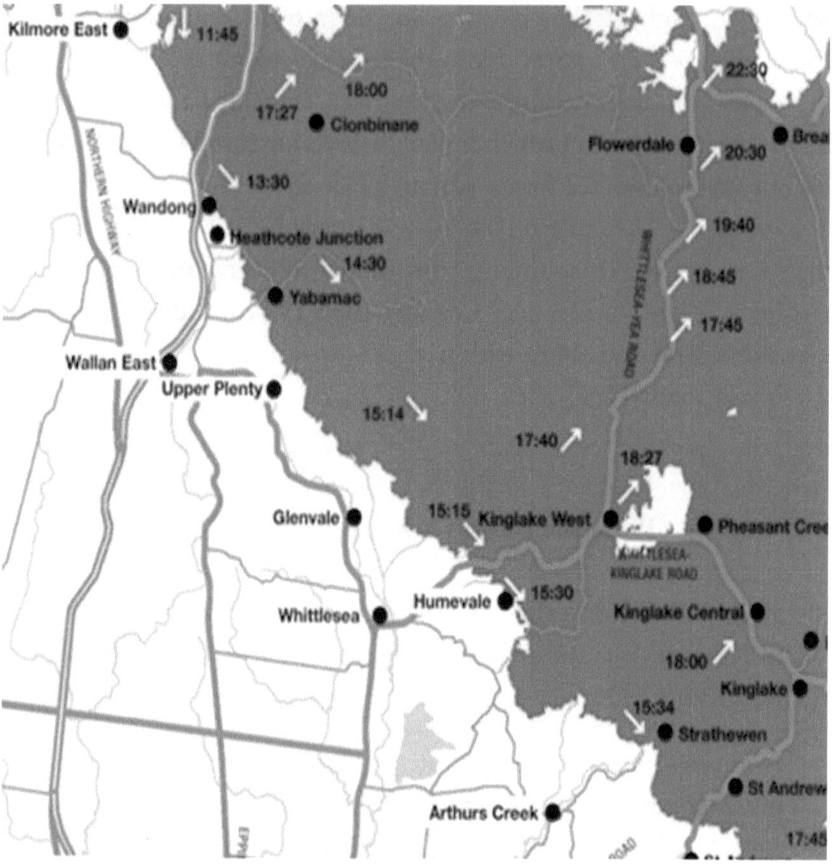

Kilmore East, where the fire began, is in the NW corner of the map. Kinglake is in the SE. Shaded areas indicate fire boundaries. Fire direction is shown by arrows. The distance From Kilmore East to Kinglake West is thirty kilometres. (Map: Royal Commission.)

※

Cameron had met Laura in heaven in Scotland. At least it seemed like heaven at the time. In fact, it was Ryan's Bar in Edinburgh, beneath the hulking and brooding presence of the historic Edinburgh Castle.

The young Aussie, fresh out of his plumbing apprenticeship in Melbourne, had been tipped into a job in the Scottish capital by relatives.

Unable to locate a Christmas party they were supposed to be at in December 1995, he and some mates found their way instead to Ryan's Bar, where Laura had promised to keep a friend company for a few minutes.

It was one of those special moments when life seems to fizz and sparkle as a young man and woman strike up a relationship over a few drinks.

Showing an amazing paucity of imagination, the local lads had nicknamed the big Aussie "Bigyin" (Scottish for Big One) and when Bigyin said "G'day, I'm Cameron" to Laura she looked at him "like I was a dickhead".

At the end of the night they went out into the fresh snow together. Christmas lights were twinkling and the castle was lit up spectacularly. It was like he had somehow found himself inside one of those glass paperweights that come alive with snow when you turn them upside down and shake them. It was so cold Cameron lent Laura his coat to keep warm and she hailed a taxi and disappeared into the night.

Cameron went back inside for another shot of liquid courage then decided to chance his arm. He jumped in a cab and went to Laura's place. Among other things, he wanted the coat back. Fourteen years later they had two boys together and a daughter, Sian, from Laura's previous relationship.

Laura had sacrificed her Edinburgh career to live among the farms and dirt roads of Pheasant Creek where it was 46 degrees with a bushfire on the move.

❧

Cam, Laura and the boys settled back to relax in the delicious cool air of his parents' house but as Cameron gazed out the west-facing windows he caught his first sight of that smoke from the Kilmore East fire. He went outside for a better view. Laura and the boys followed and the four of them watched the plume grow larger.

Cam and Ross reached the same conclusion about the same time;

northerly winds would most likely push the fire around the bottom of the mountain, if it ever got that far. The mushrooming cloud of smoke was the problem of some other unfortunates and Kinglake would stay clear of the threat.

However, they, and everyone else at Kinglake, were unaware of what was happening behind the scenes.

From the Bushfires Royal Commission

Even when more staff arrived at Kilmore Incident Control Centre they were still under- qualified to handle the disaster that was about to confront them.

1.00 P.M. Kinglake West National Park ranger Tony Fitzgerald was told by a superior that the Kilmore ICC wasn't functioning very well and you are on your own.

1.58 P.M. The fire crossed Australia's major highway, the Hume, at Heathcote Junction, about twenty-five kilometres from Kinglake West. By now it was burning on a front three kilometres wide.

Ross was most concerned about Bec; it was possible that Whittlesea would be in the fire's path. She had already told him on the mobile phone that festival organisers were checking their bushfire emergency plans.

At 3.30 P.M. Ross phoned Bec again. The situation was becoming more urgent, with the CFA website predicting Whittlesea would come under ember attack by 5.30 P.M. Bec assured him the main road out of town to the south, which took people back towards Melbourne, was safe but they were worried about the campers who were beginning to argue with organisers and demand they be allowed to leave the site.

She said winds coming off the fires were extraordinarily hot. It was like sitting inside a convection oven. The two of them agreed it was time to activate the Buchanan fire plan, just in case.

That meant it was time to get ready to leave.

What Ross couldn't see from his house on the southern slope of the Kinglake ridge was a second plume of smoke rising ominously from the forest at Murrindindi to the north-east.

Cameron Caine had seen it; he was filling a kettle at the kitchen window of his parents' house when his heart sank. He placed the kettle down and stared at the expanding balloon of white smoke on the blue horizon. Cam feared there was a greater risk the northerly winds would push this second fire towards Kinglake.

Hot winds were surging across the state, the mercury was heading skyward into unfamiliar territory (46.4 degrees) and the humidity was akin to desert conditions you'd find on Australia's parched Nullarbor Plain. It was all conducive to the perfect firestorm.

Cam ran outside and phoned his mate and colleague, Senior Constable Roger Wood. Roger was working one-up and was already on his way to Murrindindi. The mobile phone reception was patchy and the last words Cameron heard before the line dropped out were "the shit's hit the fan".

This second fire was about thirty kilometres in a direct line from Kinglake, not far when wild winds were gusting so strongly that trees were cracking and branches were snapping like twigs.

Cameron yelled for Laura to come and take a look. There was no sense of urgency yet but the new blaze was something to keep an eye on.

His phone rang, he was hoping it was Roger calling back with more news from Murrindindi but instead it was the tradesman who had now fixed the aircon.

As the Caines piled into the car and headed for home along the ridge they noticed that the smoke plume from the Kilmore East blaze had grown enormous; it turned the sun blood red and stained everything with a sinister orange glow. That orange glow is the hallmark of Australian bushfires. You don't need to see the flames or smell the smoke to know there's a fire somewhere. The ghostly shroud of altered light that descends on the mountains and valleys is enough to set the heart racing. People know immediately there's a wildfire loose somewhere.

Some radio news reports now placed the Kilmore East fire at Hidden Valley, only about twenty kilometres away.

Cameron had a quick shower around 5 P.M. and as he was towelling himself dry the power blacked out. Everything went quiet, save for the continued roaring of the winds in the nearby trees and yells from the kids who wanted to know who turned the TV off.

The Caines live in a secluded little valley at Pheasant Creek, in between Kinglake West and Kinglake. There's one close neighbour but mostly they are surrounded by farmland. A small stream, dotted with tree ferns and mountain ash, forms one idyllic boundary line. It's their rural refuge, a safe and gentle place to raise their children.

From down in their valley they had seen only clear blue sky when they arrived home earlier. Any fire threat from the fires to the north-west or the north-east remained extremely remote. Nevertheless, Cameron decided to start work early to help Roger Wood. He put on his uniform and then reassured Laura that if either of the fires got close enough to worry about then the whole family would shelter at the police station in Kinglake. In the meantime, they could simply switch on the generator and watch TV in air-conditioned safety.

He kissed Laura goodbye and headed out the backdoor only to be stopped in his tracks by a spectacular broiling mass of muddy smoke that was heading their way from the south as the winds began to swing around. It was as eerie as it was sudden, and it was coming from a direction they hadn't anticipated.

A brown twilight was enveloping them.

Even so Cameron was still more concerned about the fire in the north-east at Murrindindi, which is the direction the flames had come from three years earlier. There was no way the Kilmore East blaze, or any other fire, was going to race up the hill from the south, it just didn't happen like that.

He told Laura it would be four or five hours before the Murrindindi blaze reached them, assuming it didn't change direction in the meantime.

Cameron set off for work in his little Toyota ute at around 5.20 P.M. Amazingly, although he could see masses of smoke violently churning and heaving and occasionally blocking out the sun to his south, he couldn't smell it. He was confident it was a fair way off, although he guessed it was going to be a long and tough shift.

The senior constable pulled out onto the main Kinglake-Whittlesea Road, and his eye caught what seemed to be an extraordinary sunset filtering through the trees and smoke. Then the sunset flickered and moved. His heart missed a beat.

It was flames. Incredibly, the fire was coming from the south and it was almost on them.

CHAPTER 2

A FIRE TSUNAMI

THE BUCHANANS LIVE about four kilometres from the Caines, on the opposite side of the Kinglake ridge, the south side.

Although the CFA website was still warning only of threats to Whittlesea, Ross was worried about Kinglake West. He made the decision at 4.00 p.m. to take Macca and Aiden to Kinglake, about eighteen kilometres away, so they would be with Neeve and their grandparents and out of harm's way.

At the bottom of the mountain people were becoming scared. From the Whittlesea football oval Bec could see, hear and feel the fire heading their way. In the distance to the north-west trees were exploding into flames.

Bec was also in regular contact with eldest son Calum at the Kinglake store. Staff, and customers, were monitoring a two-way radio which accessed the CFA frequencies, so they had as much idea as anybody about how the disaster was unfolding.

In the meantime, festival organisers decided they had no option: they had to evacuate the campers. There was a waft of panic in the air but then, just as the runaway fire front was bearing down on a township of five thousand people, it changed direction. As the winds began to swing around to the south the fire headed up the heavily timbered mountain towards Bec's home.

She watched as fire trucks impotently trailed the raging flames. None could stand in front of such a formidable enemy. Bec rang her father Mick Clark in Kinglake and told him the fire was heading up the hill. It was the only warning they received. Bec and the Clarks were on the top of the warning-tree for their respective streets. When the alert came from the CFA that a fire was on its way they were supposed to call others, who in turn would phone more neighbours.

The calls never came.

Meanwhile, Ross realised it was time to get Macca and Aiden out. He piled them, their dog Jazz, family photos and business papers into the car and raced down to the Clarks' Kinglake house. When they arrived at the Reserve Road home Mick was in the backyard dampening down the grass and garden. He was using an electric pump to draw water from an underground basin. Mick also had a pump hooked up to the water tank. That pump was driven by petrol, not electricity, so he was well prepared if there was a power blackout.

CFA staff had dubbed the Clarks' brick house the safest in the street. It was only about 300 metres away from the apparent security of the Kinglake shopping strip.

In contrast, the whole of National Park Road where the Buchanans lived was classified as not defendable if threatened by a bushfire. The forest edged up close to the Buchanans' back fence, and further down, off to the side of the road, the mountain dropped away in steep and spectacular valleys and gorges that attracted bushwalkers from the city.

Months after the fire the Royal Commission heard that the floor of this eucalypt forest contained up to 50 tonnes of combustible debris per hectare. It was disaster fodder waiting for a spark.

Ross has never doubted for one minute he made the right decision to leave his children with their grandparents.

Ignoring speed limits, he rushed back to Kinglake West just in case he had to defend his home against a fire of uncertain intensity arriving from an unknown direction. There was no information on the internet, radio or TV about the precise location of the threat. Smoke was starting to thicken but the sun was still visible. It was impossible to tell where the smoke was coming from but it looked a considerable way off.

At 4.30 p.m., the CFA website still warned only of impending ember attack at Whittlesea so his thoughts were with Bec and how she was coping with the evacuations. No one on the Kinglake ridge had any official warning that the fire was almost on them.

Across the road a neighbour, Helen Barlow, asked for help to start up her pump system. Ross got it going but in a sure sign the fire was approaching, he noticed the smoke plume was getting bigger. He raced inside to put on some heavy clothing, and then the power went down, taking the internet with it. Having decided to stay and fight, Ross had no idea of what he was facing. If the CFA website had been right he had no immediate concerns. But within seconds he found out that the CFA site was barely telling half the story.

Back outside he could now clearly see flames for the first time, they were coming in from the north-west! He swore to himself but didn't panic.

The Kilmore East blaze had driven spot-fires around the foot of the mountain toward Whittlesea and also across the mountains, and it seemed the front was broader than he expected. Worse was to come moments later.

As he prepared to defend his house a Department of Sustainability and Environment ranger, Tony Fitzgerald, pulled up. The adrenaline was obviously pumping but Tony remained calm and measured.

He warned Ross that in Pine Ridge Road further south towards the national park gates "everything is on fire, houses are gone". Tony added that he couldn't tell Ross what to do, but if he was in the same situation he'd "get out fast".

So Ross knew the fire was coming from the north-west because he could see the flames, but now it was also bearing down from the south as the surging winds began to swing around and push it up the hill from Whittlesea.

What Ross and the others who initially stayed behind to fight couldn't know was that this deadly fire maelstrom had already claimed the lives of former TV newsreader Brian Naylor, his wife Moiree and others on the far side of the national park to the south-west. Their fate had been sealed by the extreme intensity of that wind change. They had been preparing to face the bushfire from the north-west but the conflagration had spread along the base of the mountain behind them near Whittlesea and was now also being pushed up the hill from the southerly direction.

Ross heeded the ranger's advice and went inside to collect as many family belongings as he could carry. He was then stunned to discover that in the potentially fatal two minutes he'd turned his back on the fire, it had surrounded the property.

For the moment the option to leave was gone.

It was about half an hour between the time Ross saw those first flames from the north-west and Cam encountering fire from the south as the winds began to change. The senior constable was torn between loyalty to his job and the community, and love of his family. He was anxious that the fire could close in behind him as he drove to Kinglake, cutting him off from Laura and the kids.

He rang Laura's mobile phone, but reception was bad. Cam screamed at his wife to "get out, get the kids… get the fuck out now… try and make it to the police station".

The phone connection spluttered in and out, then went dead.

As the southerly weather change hit Melbourne after five o'clock the temperature plunged one degree per minute over a fifteen-minute period. But in keeping with the day's extreme weather theme, this change was not like the ones which traditionally spell the end of a heatwave and bring relief to millions of Victorians. This was a dry change with just a few spots of rain here and there. Normally the cooler conditions are accompanied by showers which dampen the summer flames and signal to exhausted firefighters that an old friend has arrived.

That's the way it's always been.

But not only was this southerly change a dry one, it also rode in on the back of howling winds.

People have a way of recalling where they were when major events happen, for example the death of Princess Diana or the destruction of the Twin Towers. Likewise, many Victorians will never forget the moment that fearsome southerly change roared across their state late in the afternoon on February 7.

Trees that had been battered by northerlies of at least 80 kilometres an hour now bent over in the face of winds of equal strength from the other direction. It was a tempest not meant to mix with flames.

Cameron Caine made the decision not to turn around and head home. He was certain Laura had heard his warning to get out, and based on his experiences of the 2006 fires she would have ample time to pack and leave.

In fact, as he drove closer to Kinglake township he had to remind himself to stay calm and stay in control. There were no more flames in Kinglake, just some small smoke columns in the distance to the south. It was business as usual in the township, except there was no power. Cameron opened up the police station and started the generator. He then called Roger to find out what was happening at Murrindindi.

But Roger was no longer at the north-eastern fire; he'd turned around after learning the Kilmore East blaze was now threatening the Kinglake ridge.

There was stress in Roger's voice as he urged Cam to "bring a car to Kinglake West. Jo's rung and there's fire near the house. I'll go home from here".

Jo is Roger's wife and as his shift was coming to an end he was eager to get home to her. They live at St Andrews, about twenty minutes to the south of Kinglake village. Cameron was stunned. St Andrews was on the other side of Whittlesea, the east side, a long way from Kilmore.

Was it a separate blaze or had one of the two big fires somehow "spotted" their way across the mountain?

He quickly kitted-up, jumped in the old ute and headed back to Kinglake West. In the rear view mirror he caught a glimpse of Kinglake's main street. It was about 5.40 p.m.; people were in the street as normal and the sky was blue. It was the last time he'd see his township intact. Within forty minutes the gusting southerly winds would drive the fire from St Andrews, and elsewhere, up over the mountain obliterating everything in its path.

The thing about old utes is that seldom does everything in them work. In the case of Cam's car it was the driver side window that wouldn't stay up. The cab began to fill with smoke and the heat was becoming unbearable.

What Cam didn't realise as he headed to Kinglake West and drove past the National Park Road turn off was that barely two minutes away Ross Buchanan and other residents were already fighting to save their homes, and their lives.

Earlier, at five o'clock, Calum Buchanan had finished his shift at the Kinglake store and he wanted to get home. The oldest Buchanan boy was aware of fire threats at the western end of the Kinglake ridge, but inside the store, and in the township itself, people were mostly calm.

Customers at the Kinglake hardware store and petrol station recall that late in the afternoon people were listening to a CFA monitor. Some of the firies sounded like they were in life-threatening situations.

One call warned "mayday, overburn". It was the international distress call.

Nine times a desperate firefighter made that chilling "mayday, over-burn" call.

In fact it was the Kinglake West tanker urgently calling for help only minutes after newsreader Brian Naylor had told the crew he was ready to defend his own property. Firefighter Glen Barlow says their distress calls were never acknowledged, which has led to concerns that the CFA communication system failed. Glen is the husband of Helen Barlow, who was preparing to fight the flames alongside Ross.

At one stage the West crew huddled inside their truck and were separated from their captain by a sheet of flame. Miraculously they all managed to survive.

≼

Calum heard from Bec that a fire in National Park Road was burning near their home. He rang up his dad and begged him to leave, and "don't forget the laptop".

Ross said it was too late to get out and he was staying to defend their property. Unbeknown to Ross, as soon as his son finished work he and young mate Kevin Smith attempted to drive down National Park Road to help but were pushed back by flames.

Bec also called to check on her husband but Ross was desperately manning the hoses and sprinklers and had no time to talk to her. He couldn't see more than twenty metres because of the smoke, although he was vaguely aware of eucalypts combusting as if flamethrowers had been pointed at them. There were also explosions in the distance.

Next door neighbour Wally Spezza and his 15-year-old son Chris, Macca's best mate, were trying to keep the flames away from their house, while across the road Helen was fighting the fire with the pump Ross had fixed earlier in the day.

Ross knew the CFA trucks wouldn't be coming to his help, but where were the fire bombers and the helicopters they'd seen in action in 2006? Aircraft had in fact been requested as early as 12.30 p.m. that day but were ineffective because of the massive amount of smoke blanketing the region.

From his backyard Ross could see young Chris Spezza on the roof of their home courageously trying to douse the flames with a hose.

Chris was being showered by embers and was also dodging dangerous fireballs that the gusting winds were hurling in his direction. The fireballs broke free from a large conifer tree that was shredded by the scorching flames and winds.

Wally left them and ran across the road to check on Helen, who'd been joined by two other people. All three were huddled under the carport with their hoses. A paddock of cleared land behind her house was the only thing saving it from destruction. Wally noticed his garage was on fire, the galvanised iron seemed to be burning. It looked as if the air itself was burning. How could that be, he wondered?

Again the sky turned black and it was like a mini tornado of smoke and fire and wind was circling their houses and bearing down on them. Wally then saw something he'll never forget, something that was emblematic of the helplessness of humans on that catastrophic day.

Ross was standing in his backyard, where it meets the national park; a diminutive figure with a humble hose in his hand. Monster flames, so huge that from Wally's vantage point he couldn't see the top of them, were shooting into the darkened sky.

The flames were consuming the almost twenty-metre-high tree canopy, and the fire seared off at least that distance again before disappearing into the smoke. It was a tsunami made of fire, not water, and it was as if their homes were helpless yachts trying to survive in a sea of flames.

No sooner would they hose down one spot fire in the backyard than another would spring up elsewhere as those gale force winds applied a monster hair dryer to the dampened areas.

It was becoming hopeless. Wally screamed out to Ross that they had to get out. He described Ross's expression as a look that said "I'd just stared at hell". Ross dropped the hose and ran.

He grabbed the laptop, the cat, the bird and a few other items and leapt into his panel van.

All afternoon Ross had been focused on saving their home, now his concentration turned to saving his own life as he backed the van out into National Park Road. His window was about one third down and the cat, in keeping with the contrary nature of its species, leapt through the gap and sprinted back towards the house.

With flames burning on his property Ross cursed and then gave chase. Minutes seemed like hours as he pursued the cat with fire burning all around him. He gave up but as he jumped back in the van, he noticed that the grass was on fire around Bec's car, which she left behind when she was given a ride to Whittlesea that morning. Ross decided to leave the van and save the other vehicle.

He headed off down National Park Road not knowing where Wally or Helen were. In fact, he hardly knew where Ross Buchanan was. The smoke was so thick that he could barely see the road in front so he hunched himself over the steering wheel and focused on the barely visible white line as it snaked its way under his front bumper. He may have been in the middle of the road but at least he was escaping.

Later he was to learn that other cars had turned into National Park Road, also using the white line as a beacon but heading in the opposite direction to him. As fate would have it, he missed them.

Ross also got an attack of the guilts. While fleeing the fire with flames on both sides of the road all he could think of was the CFA cardinal warning about not leaving it too late to get out. If he perished his friends would think him a fool. He thought about turning around and heading back to the house, but with visibility down to one or two metres and walls of yellow to the left and right that would have been tantamount to a death wish.

Ross was virtually driving blind. A glance at the speedometer showed he was doing 20 kilometres an hour. It felt too fast. His nerves were jangling. It wasn't fast enough. He struggled to keep the car on the road. That was partly because there were no lines demarcating the edge of the asphalt from the gravel and partly because he couldn't see the white line in the middle properly because it blended into the smoke. It occurred to him that yellow paint would have been better.

But as he pushed on, the flames receded and by the time he reached the main road the tsunami was gone and he was in calm water. At the intersection Ross turned left, the opposite direction to Kinglake, and found a bunch of people had gathered at the post office, including a mate called Kiwi, who had already lost his house in National Park Road.

He and Kiwi had a beer. No one had much idea what was going on, they certainly didn't realise that the fire was still coming for them.

From the Bushfires Royal Commission

1.40 P.M. – A fire prediction map, based on line scans by an aircraft an hour earlier, was produced at the Emergency Control Centre headquarters in Melbourne. It was not passed on to Kilmore ICC.

2.13 P.M. – Burnt leaves fell at the Kangaroo Ground fire tower, to the south of Kinglake, about fifty kilometres from where the blaze began.

2.20 P.M. – a CFA officer at the Kangaroo Ground Incident Control Centre concluded that Kinglake and nearby communities were in the path of the fire and he prepared "urgent threat" messages. However, he was unable to contact his superiors, and the warnings were never sent. Under CFA protocol the warnings could only be sent from Kilmore ICC.

An information officer, with the training to compose and disseminate warnings to the media, arrived at Kilmore ICC at 3.30 P.M. She was seated away from the management team which was under immense stress. She didn't have a computer or a printer.

3.30 p.m. – many communities were in deep trouble. Fire was running up gullies to the south of Kinglake West and was also approaching that community from the north-west. Fires were also noted in the gullies to the south-east of Kinglake West.

4.10 p.m. – the information officer at Kilmore ICC began preparing urgent warnings but she was unable to distribute them because she didn't have a fax machine.

4.30 p.m. – a senior CFA career officer arrived at Kilmore ICC to take charge.

CHAPTER 3

ON THE RUN

CHAOS ABOUNDED.

Cameron Caine headed along the main road towards Kinglake West CFA. Again and again he tried to call Laura to check that she and the boys had evacuated, but the phone was always busy or there was simply no reception.

When he arrived at the CFA building Roger was waiting for him. It was about 6 P.M. Senior Constable Wood had just been at the Whittlesea-Yea Road intersection about four kilometres away to the west and the fire had already been through there.

Cam began to get a glimpse of the looming crisis. He'd seen flames to the south of the main road and there were more blazes on the Whittlesea-Yea Road to the west and down at the bottom of the hill at St Andrews to the south-east.

They were almost surrounded, and who knew what the Murrindindi fire in the north-east was doing or where it was. Neither officer was aware that people had already perished only kilometres away or that Ross and others on the southern side of the ridge had fled for their lives.

Roger listened in to a message on the radio; there was a four-car pile-up on the main road back towards Kinglake. Cameron was incredulous;

he'd just travelled along that road from the police station and hadn't seen any accidents.

Roger took off and Cam followed in the white ute. With a growing sense of despair, he kept trying to call Laura.

They sped through Pheasant Creek and past the turn off to his home.

Up ahead, near where he'd first seen flames on his way to work, a grey wall had descended on the road and through this seemingly impenetrable mass of smoke cars were making their escape from Kinglake.

A whole line of traffic was emerging through the wall.

Cameron began to feel sick. What if Laura and the boys had evacuated to the police station and were now in danger? What if they'd been caught in the smoke and then cars had blindly cannoned into each other? Or worse, what if he'd sent them directly into the path of the fire?

He kept dialling.

Roger waited for a gap in the line of traffic then did a U-turn and headed west again. Cam followed the police car to the Pheasant Creek general store at the top of the Caines' road. Some cars were already parked there, and when the police vehicle arrived others began to stop as well. Soon there were vehicles spilling out of the car park and lining both sides of the road.

Cam left the ute beside the general store and joined Roger in the police car. One of his neighbours ran over to them, she'd been trying to escape on various roads but they were all cut off by fire. She told the two police officers they were surrounded by walls of flame.

More cars pulled in as people began to sense there was safety in numbers, or failing that, at least the police officers would know what to do. But Cameron's immediate focus was on his family and just as he was asking his neighbour if she'd seen Laura and the kids he experienced something he'd never quite felt before.

Laura pulled up in the traffic. Tension gushed from his body in an overwhelming flood of relief. He rushed to them and hugged her and the boys tightly.

While he felt their warmth and their life through his uniform, dozens of others were dying at that very moment at Kinglake. It was about 6.15 p.m.

※

Laura had received Cameron's broken message, "Get out now and head for the police station."

As she activated the family's fire plan of getting photos together and grabbing the dog, eldest son Angus walked in and said, "Have you seen outside?" It had gone muddy dark. Laura's adrenaline began to pump.

She had to get out quickly but there was no way she was leaving without her treasured photo of "Old Scotland" which sat proudly above the fireplace. "Old Scotland" wouldn't budge; the damn picture was snagged on a hook. Laura used up valuable minutes struggling with it.

Eventually she loaded "Old Scotland" into the car along with photo albums, the pet Jack Russell terrier and her two boys. By now it was so dark she had to turn on the car lights so she could see the driveway. Laura estimated the time at around 6 p.m. The fire was close but she didn't know how close.

Angus sat in the passenger seat, a tone of panic in his voice. "What are we going to do?" he asked. Laura explained that they were all going to stay calm and try and navigate their way out along the narrow dirt road.

Huge mountain ash trees loomed on both sides of the road. Laura asked Angus to watch for broken branches or logs that might block their escape. The road wasn't wide enough for her to execute a U-turn and she feared they could be trapped in the car.

Laura's eyes strained to find the road among the dense smoke; by now she couldn't see further than a metre in front of the car bonnet. Even without the frightening prospect of flames descending on them it was a perilously dangerous ride.

Four-year-old Harry was in the back seat cuddling Boo, the dog. The younger boy kept repeating "I'm scared, Mummy, I'm scared." Laura reassured him that it was okay, they were all together.

As they slowly made their way towards the Pheasant Creek store Angus startled Laura by yelling "I can see flames Mum, Mum I can see flames!" Harry could tell by the fear in his brother's voice that the situation was urgent and he began sobbing in terror.

"Where can you see the flames?" Laura asked. "Right there, right beside the car, Mum. Look!"

Yes! Laura could see sheets of flame! She was driving right through the fire but she couldn't allow herself the luxury of feeling scared; she had to focus all her energies on getting her boys to safety. "You watch the fire, Angus, and I'll watch the road."

She drove with flames licking at the vehicle until gradually in the distance she began to see headlights, and eventually the Pheasant Creek store came into view. Then Laura could even see Cameron standing in the middle of the intersection!

Looking back now she thinks it's a miracle they made it out. Ironically, if she hadn't taken so long to evacuate, if "Old Scotland" hadn't clung to the wall so obstinately, Laura and the boys may have turned left at the Pheasant Creek store as she looked for her husband. She would have driven into the holocaust.

As Cam looked around he could see there were dozens of cars gathered outside the store. People began descending on him and Roger asking for help.

Pheasant Creek general store stood across the road from an old plantation crowded with fifteen-metre tall pine trees. The store had a petrol bowser and a cage full of LPG bottles. The two police officers realised that it would be suicide to stay put.

They could now also hear the fire approaching; it was screeching like the jet engines on a 747. They had to yell to be heard. The officers knew they had to do something, but they didn't know in which direction to go to find safety. Roger decided he'd take the police car back to Kinglake West CFA to check if the road was safe.

As Roger and the vehicle disappeared down the main road Cam was left standing by himself feeling very much alone. He looked anxiously at all the people outside the store. A few more cars and their desperate drivers arrived. The people assumed Cam and Roger had some idea what was happening. They assumed incorrectly. A vague thought that they could all perish in a chaotic and fiery inferno began gathering strength somewhere in the back of Cam's mind.

The roar of the fire became louder and the southerly change sending it in their direction was so strong that the tail of Cam's police shirt was flapping about like it was on a flagpole.

Suddenly it went even darker and the back of Cam's neck bristled. Cars had their lights on and people were turned into brown silhouettes. He couldn't see the fire but he knew it must be close.

His mobile phone rang. It was Roger. The road to Kinglake West was still clear but they had to move quickly. If Cam was a religious man he would have thanked God there and then.

Across the main road the pine trees began to pop and crackle. It sounded like weapons were being discharged. He yelled at people to drive to Kinglake West CFA. Cam noticed a young guy by himself in a white van; he sprinted over and asked the driver to wait until the others had gone. They would leave together at the rear of the convoy.

Back in the middle of the main road Cam kept screaming at people to head west, but the cars seemed to trickle out ever so slowly. They were taking an eternity to clear the car park and from the approaching noise in the pine forest Cam could tell the fire was almost on them.

Another guy in a twin cab ute was towing a large trailer and needed to do a u-turn to join the convoy. Cam was worried the man might struggle with the turn and block the main road for precious seconds, or even minutes. He asked the driver to wait and let others through. The guy ignored him, a sense of self-preservation kicking in, but there was nothing Cam could do; the police uniform meant nothing.

Smoke was so thick it was affecting their breathing. That vague thought about the prospects of them all dying loomed even larger in his mind. He now believed there was a very good chance many people would be burned to death along with him, and his family, right there at Pheasant Creek.

The twin cab ute and trailer made the turn and Cam kept yelling "move, move, move" to the remaining cars.

Now the roar was so loud it was almost impossible to hear anything else. It was as if the deadly and malevolent fire was deliberately pushing the terrifying noise ahead of itself to instil fear in its victims.

As the last of the cars departed Cam jumped into the white van. He re-assessed his survival odds and decided they'd worsened significantly. It was now highly likely he was going to die. It was terrifying. He thought his number was up, the fire was that close.

Just as they sped away something almost unbelievable happened. Two Toyota Land Cruisers emerged through the smoke. They were towing horse floats! Cam frantically signalled and screamed at them to follow. He looked behind to check they'd joined the convoy. What he saw sent the shivers through him again. Huge flames were now arching over a bus shelter and crossing the road where he'd been standing just moments before. The fire was reaching out for the Pheasant Creek store.

Still, they weren't safe yet, embers were igniting bush along both sides of the road. It was as if a gigantic invisible hand was throwing fire in their direction, setting scrub and trees alight spontaneously.

They found themselves driving through a kilometre long tunnel of fire.

More people, including Ross Buchanan, milled about the car park at the Kinglake West post office. The white van slowed and Cam made sure those people knew where everyone was heading. He just hoped it was to safety.

Dozens of thoughts were racing through his mind but as he slumped back in the seat those thoughts were all crowded out by one overwhelming emotion: relief. He and his family were alive.

Pheasant Creek bus shelter, where Cam almost lost his life. (Pic: Police Life.*)*

CHAPTER 4

THE FIGHT OF THEIR LIVES

IF THE FIRE was a carnivorous beast, instead of just a metaphoric one, it would have been accused of tormenting its prey on February 7.

The two people who had been with Helen Barlow helping to save her home in National Park Road leapt into a car and drove off.

Helen, Wally and Chris then loaded her two cats and a dog into their cars and got ready to make a run for it. The dense black smoke was so thick they couldn't even see across the road, so they drove over to pick up Ross.

He was gone!

Now as they looked around them they were surrounded by flames. It was too late to get out. They fled back to Helen's house with a sense of panic creeping over them. Then, miraculously, it went calm. Smoke cleared and the sun came out. It occurred to Wally that it was the first time all day he'd been glad to see the damn sun.

A National Parks crew arrived with fear in their eyes; they'd been further south and had seen the holocaust sweeping up the hill. They knew something huge was heading their way because even before they could see the flames they noticed that leaves and debris were being sucked towards the fire.

They had made a run for it in their vehicles but the 4WD that ranger Tony Fitzgerald was driving caught fire. Fitzgerald said it was like the car had been hit by "a ball of radiant heat". Flames were streaming from the tyres. The ranger and his fellow workers had fled to his nearby house where they tried to shelter until the wind blew the roof off and it caught fire. They retreated further along National Park Road with houses literally exploding beside them.

After warning Helen, Wally and Chris that there were more flames coming, the crew continued towards the main road until the fire caught them again. They survived by parking the 4WDs in a paddock and digging a hole between the vehicles to provide some cover.

In the meantime, Wally and the other two turned their energies to damping out the smaller spot fires until suddenly it began turning ominously dark again. Wally's gut tightened. He knew straight away "the sun was retreating and the beast was coming back".

This time it felt like the fire was encircling them as it decided what it would take next. Except now it wasn't a vertical wall, it was coming at them horizontally. The flames were running sideways and screeching like an aircraft.

Wally ran into the middle of the road and there, only centimetres in front of him, emerging out of the soupy thick smoke was a human face. It was the spookiest thing he'd ever seen. The face was shrouded in a hood which was giving off smoke and small flames.

Soon a second face appeared, and then two more. There were two adults and two children covered by smouldering blankets.

They scared some of the life out of him.

Incredibly they'd managed to walk and run from near the entry gates at the national park. As soon as one house caught fire they'd fled to another to seek shelter. The fire tracked them all the way up National Park Road.

They'd run the gauntlet of hell and survived.

Wally took them into Helen's house where another six people had also appeared seeking shelter. Thirteen of them now, about to fight for their lives.

An asthmatic girl was highly distressed so Chris took her and some of the others downstairs where it was easier to breathe. He helped them with wet towels and water while outside five adults, including Wally and Helen, battled to save the house.

The smoke was so dense that when they had trouble breathing they lay down in the dirt to suck in the cleaner air. Soon enough the water was all gone and they were exhausted. As tired as they were they knew that if they stopped fighting they would die. So they fought on, for more than three enervating hours, then when the battle was finally won they collapsed together and watched their neighbours' houses burning to the ground.

Later Chris and Wally lay side by side on the scorched driveway. Wally confided to his teenage son that his life would never be the same. The boy told his dad "you're my hero". "No way, you're my hero!" said Wally. "I did what a father was expected to do, you did so much more than anyone could expect from a 15-year-old."

It was a magic moment between the father and son. Time slipped away, but within the hour it would catch them again. Chris would learn his best mate, Macca, was dead.

※

From the top of the crest before he reached Kinglake West CFA and the primary school, Cam was confronted by an extraordinary sight. Before him stretched a long line of cars and on his left, to the south, houses and sheds were erupting in flames. Nearby in National Park Road Wally and the others were trying to stay alive.

Cam began to take stock of what he was seeing, he had no idea what the bigger picture looked like but the immediate confusion and destruction was akin to a battlefield. That's an analogy he was to draw on continually over the next twenty-four hours, particularly when he realised there were numerous victims in this one-sided fight.

It was 6.45 p.m. and although the sun was still high in the sky over the western horizon, it was like twilight on the Kinglake ridge.

Outside the CFA building Cameron stared in disbelief, a milling crowd of up to 300 people was there. They were relying on Cam and Roger, and a handful of CFA and other volunteers, to know what to do. But Cam only knew two things: his family was safe and he had absolutely no idea what was going to happen next.

Flames to the south of the Kinglake West CFA building. (Pic: Helen Barlow.)

Sian's story

If only Cameron knew.

Cam and Laura weren't worried about their 19-year-old daughter, she'd been seen driving in Whittlesea earlier in the day and although they couldn't contact her on the phone they were confident she was out of harm's way.

Sian had indeed been in Whittlesea as she and a Kinglake netball friend, Annie Lucas, took a guy home to nearby Doreen. They could see smoke in the distance but Annie reassured Sian that, just like last time, it would be a week before fire reached them.

Sian returned to Pheasant Creek midafternoon to find her family had gone out, so she went back to Annie's place, less than a kilometre away.

Beryl Lucas, Annie's mother, told her the fire had swept into Humevale, which is outside Whittlesea and not far from where they were driving only an hour or so before. Still, there was nothing on the radio or internet to indicate they were under any kind of direct threat.

Very late in the afternoon she heard a car screech to a stop in the Lucas's driveway. They went to investigate and were stunned to see flames coming from the direction of the Pheasant Creek general store. To the left more flames were heading in their direction from Kinglake. The man in the car, a friend of the Lucas family, frantically told them that he'd already lost his house to the marauding fire and he'd come to help them.

John and Beryl Lucas had a diesel generator which sucked water from their dam and fed two hoses. The Lucas family was ready for a fight. Beryl ordered Sian and Annie to go inside and fill the bath with water then sit in it and cover themselves with a wet blanket. They did as they were told and noticed as they headed indoors that the day had turned to night as a mass of smoke enveloped them. Then came the flames.

Sian and Annie huddled in the bath as the fire lit up the house in an unnatural glimmer. Above them a skylight glowed yellow, and they could feel the fire's heat through the plastic. They could also feel the heat invading the house through the lounge room windows, which were ten metres away. The young women had no way of knowing what was happening outside, if Annie's parents had survived. Nor did they know how close the house was to combusting, or what they would do if it did burst into flames.

It felt as if they were sitting in the bath for a long time, but it may have taken less than half an hour for the front to pass by them.

They all survived.

As fate would have it Laura, Angus and Harry had driven past the Lucas house only minutes before the main fire arrived without realising Sian was inside and about to have a brush with death. Now Sian's thoughts turned to her family, had they survived?

From the Bushfires Royal Commission

4.55 P.M. – power failed along the Kinglake ridge. People were left without the internet they'd been monitoring all day. Smoke was entering Kinglake from the direction of St Andrews to the south.

5.20 P.M. – a CFA officer at Kangaroo Ground ICC ignored a directive that only Kilmore could issue threat warnings and put out his own urgent warning for Kinglake and other ridge communities. However, it was too late – there was no power and consequently no TV, internet or radio other than transistor or car radios.

5.30 P.M. – embers began to fall on Kinglake.

5.43 P.M. – southerly wind change reported at the Kangaroo Ground fire tower, south of Kinglake.

5.45 P.M. – embers began burning in Kinglake.

5.55 P.M. – southerly wind gusts of up to 90 kilometres an hour recorded at Kangaroo Ground fire tower. Urgent threat messages posted on CFA website for communities from Kinglake to Flowerdale.

8.35 P.M. – an urgent threat message for Kinglake and Flowerdale was posted which warned of a fire burning in a southerly direction. (As we have seen, the wind direction changed three hours earlier and the fire was heading in a northerly direction.)

The Royal Commission was told about the confusion at the Kilmore Incident Control Centre, which prevented the issuing of urgent threat warnings for townships along the Kinglake ridge. The hearings also heard that there were no updates at all on the CFA website about any aspect of the Kilmore East fire for more than two hours between 12.40 P.M. and 2.45 P.M.

Bec, at Whittlesea, and Ross, at Kinglake West, were watching the smoke but were unaware of precisely where the fire was burning or the direction the flames were heading until it was almost on them.

The Caines, like many other families on the Kinglake ridge, were inside sheltering from the heat and had no knowledge of the looming danger.

From early afternoon on February 7 until midday on February 8, 530 phone calls were placed to the Kilmore Incident Control Centre as people desperately sought information. Sixty-four per cent of the calls went unanswered. Kangaroo Ground ICC staff called Kilmore ICC fourteen times, without answer, between 1.54 P.M. and 5.37 P.M. on February 7.

Cam busied himself getting the cars off the road. From outside the front of the Kinglake West CFA building he could see across to the Apteds fruit farm where more flames were barrelling over the hill to their west.

Because Roger had already seen fires in that direction, further out at the Whittlesea-Yea Road, they decided to stop vehicles heading off the mountain to Whittlesea. That meant that they were, effectively, cut off on the top of the ridge. They couldn't head east back to Kinglake and heading west was now totally out of the question.

Cam stood in the middle of the road and directed cars onto the verges. An elderly man drove straight at the senior constable. Cam was concerned the man couldn't see him properly in the smoke.

In fact, the driver's vision was fine and he edged forward until the front bumper made contact with Cameron's shins. He then got out, screaming, "I've spent the last hour saving my house. You can't stop me. You'll have to use that thing on your hip [Cam's gun] if you want to stop me!"

The elderly gent got back in the car and put his foot down. Cam leapt out of the way and watched the tail-lights disappear into the dirty brown and white smoke.

John Grover, the Kinglake West CFA captain then approached him with an urgent message. His pager had gone off and warned of up to twenty children trapped in the recreation room at the neighbouring primary school.

At the same time two more police cars arrived and one of the cops asked if Cam and Roger were the Kinglake officers because "all of Melbourne thinks you're dead". Cam's heart sank as he thought how worried his friends and family would be. But he had bigger issues to deal with.

The officers ran past the Kinglake West oval to the rear of the primary school.

This was Angus and Harry's school, maybe if there were kids inside he'd know them. They found the fire was already in the trees behind the buildings. With no time to lose they raced around the classrooms looking through windows but found no one. Realising the fire was waiting for them out back they rushed towards the main road and the front gate. But Cam had forgotten there were major works underway at the school and it was cut off from the road, and the safety of the CFA building, by a two-metre-high wire fence. They turned back again towards the rear where the fire was roaring and spitting flames in the school's direction.

Cam yelled at them to run for it and they sprinted out a side gate. They could feel the radiant heat from the fire and sucked in smoke as they ran back towards the refuge of the CFA building.

Sprinting past the Kinglake West oval, one of the officers noticed the grass had caught fire. It was extraordinary. The grass was only a few centimetres high but it was so dry the flames got a hold on it and began spreading under parked cars.

Again they had to move quickly, this time to clear the oval.

By 7.30 p.m. the fire had jumped the main road, and a house directly opposite was consumed by flames. The fire was all around the CFA building. People were worried, some even alarmed, but generally they remained calm. Inevitably the rumours began to spread. "Kinglake's gone. The pub is burned to the ground. The police station, the shops, the whole lot's gone," people said.

It wasn't that bad, but it was still worse than their worst nightmares.

Cam then noticed Laura holding and consoling Ross Buchanan. She looked upset. He looked completely stunned.

CHAPTER 5

CATASTROPHE

KINGLAKE WAS JUST a normal country town. Hardware store/petrol station, police station, vet, fast food outlet and a few retail odds and sods on one side of the street with the hotel, bakery, post office, supermarket, cafe, chemist and other businesses on the north side. The village was the heart of the community providing services, food and security. It was beyond belief that this concrete and brick semi-urban heart could be attacked from the outside.

Reserve Road in Kinglake is only a few hundred metres from the shops, well within walking distance for Jenny and Mick Clark if they wanted a cup of coffee, some groceries or a newspaper. They lived at Number One Reserve Road, across the main road from paddocks. Any reasonable person would take Ross Buchanan by the hand and say, "Mate, you were absolutely right to leave your kids there."

If you had to leave them anywhere on the Kinglake ridge you would surely choose the edge of the shopping centre with its wide main road, asphalt parking areas and surrounding paddocks. Of course, if you did leave your children in Reserve Road you'd leave them with Jenny and Mick and their underground water supply, sprinklers, petrol-powered water pump and brick house.

That's what the Chambers sisters thought as well. The two animal lovers ignored advice to abandon their horses as flames approached Kinglake, but when the situation became too dangerous they sought shelter with the Clarks.

Twenty-two year old Melanie and twenty-one year old Penelope joined the three Buchanan children, the children's uncle Danny Clark, and Mick and Jenny in the home as the fire crowned, jumped from tree to tree, into the township.

They were all inside the building when the radiant heat and wind literally blew in the lounge windows showering the room first with glass and then deadly embers which began to ignite. They fled to the hallway. But all too soon the fire had a hold on the house and smoke was filling the rooms so densely they had trouble seeing.

In Whittlesea Bec called her father's mobile phone one more time as she watched her magnificent mountain disappearing behind gigantic clouds of smoke. She had dialled repeatedly with no luck. Phone reception along the ridge can be flukey.

This time someone answered. It was her brother Danny. In the background Bec could hear chaos. People were screaming, dogs were barking and smoke alarms were going off.

Her heart was racing. She was terrified.

Danny said, "We're fucked, mate, it's really bad, the house is on fire." Her brother repeated, "We're fucked, there are no CFA trucks."

Bec was beginning to panic. "Can't you get out?"

Her brother's last words to her were, "Nah, we can't get out, we're surrounded."

She replied, "Do the best you can, mate!"

From the hallway Macca, Mick and Jenny led a dash for the door. They didn't know what awaited them outside but to stay inside meant certain death. In the confusion and in the blinding smoke they believed all the others were just behind them. But Aiden was the only one to follow. Jenny could feel him clinging to her.

Outside, the air was still searing hot and the flames threatened to consume them. But at least they could breathe. Macca looked around and was the first to notice Neeve and Danny and the girls hadn't made it. He couldn't leave his little sister and the others to die. In the chaos Ross and Bec's beautiful fifteen-year-old boy went back to help.

He never made it out again. Macca, Neeve, Mel, Pen and Danny lost their lives in the safest house in the street. Two weatherboard homes in Reserve Road survived.

Bec had borrowed Calum's phone that morning and she couldn't work out how to access the messages. She was so frustrated she felt like smashing it. She ran across the road to the Whittlesea fire brigade and begged them to send some trucks to Reserve Road in Kinglake. But the firies said there was no way they could get through. Bec's phone rang, it was her mother and just for a fleeting second she was relieved. But then Jenny cried these words down the phone: "The children are gone."

"What do you mean gone? Gone where?"

"We've lost the children, Macca and Neeve are dead, and so is Danny."

Bec wandered into the middle of the road and let out the sort of scream that has sent shivers down the spine of humanity for millennia. CFA and other emergency workers ran to help her. In the background a deathly shroud of smoke enveloped the Kinglake ridge.

Distraught, she headed back towards the Whittlesea football ground where friends from the organising committee found her and took her inside. The president then broke the news to the group that two of Rebecca's children and her brother had perished in the fire.

They were all dumbfounded.

Bec was numb and for the first time she posed the question that has no answer: she sobbed "Why me?"

In the background, musicians who had stayed behind because they still wanted to play, or because they'd left it too late to leave, watched on in bewildered disbelief.

Ross was frantically dialling numbers as he sheltered at the Kinglake West CFA. He was trying to locate Calum. When his own phone rang it was Bec. She was barely able to put her words together as she told Ross to go and stand with someone he knew. Ross's heart started pounding; he'd been so worried about Calum. Had his oldest boy been burned, or injured or something worse?

Ross found Laura and stood with her as Bec bravely delivered the news that any parent would sacrifice anything, perhaps even give up their own world, to avoid saying.

"Neeve, Macca and Danny have died in the fire." There was no other way to tell it.

They were just words, humble vibrations of the vocal chords transferred over an electronic phone connection, but they carried with them the weight of an eternity. They carried with them a dark chasm that could never be bridged again.

Ross wanted Bec to take the words back, to start the conversation afresh. But once spoken they became a part of his universe, words representing truths which can't ever be altered or avoided.

He was breathing heavily as he collapsed against Laura. Ross felt as if some mysterious being had reached deep inside him and ripped out part of his self that could never be reclaimed. His first thoughts focused on denial. It had to be a mistake. They were in Kinglake; it's not possible that people were dying in the township! The township where he sent them while he now stood alive and breathing in Laura's supportive arms.

Cam went over to see why Laura and Ross were so distressed.

Through tears his wife delivered the bleak news. "How?" asked Cam.

"Because I sent them to the in-laws in Kinglake," Ross replied.

It came laced with bitterness and misplaced guilt.

Cameron felt pains in his chest as he grabbed Ross and embraced him. They sobbed in each other's arms.

"I'm so sorry" were the only words Cam could bring himself to utter. I'm so sorry.

I'm sorry, I'm sorry.

Oh God, I'm so sorry.

Words Ross and Bec were to hear spoken hundreds of times in the months ahead by hundreds of people, many of whom they didn't know.

Words they'll hear for years to come until there's space between the darkness of February 7 and whatever new lives the four remaining members of the family come to live. By then people meeting the Buchanans will still experience sorrow in their hearts but will no longer feel emotionally compelled to reach out and offer support.

It seems sadly inadequate that the best we can offer when confronted by the mystery of death is to tell a fellow human "I'm sorry". For those unwilling to accept religion's answers to life's riddles there's nothing else. No spiritual comfort, no reassuring thoughts of an afterlife. Just emptiness where loved ones once loved back.

The fact is we're a whole lot more than "sorry". Words just can't express it.

෴

When Wally and Chris Spezza arrived at Kinglake West CFA they were shocked at the size of the crowd. Wally began searching for Ross, he hadn't seen his mate since telling him it was time to flee the fire.

Wally asked a friend if he knew where Ross was. The guy had the look of death on his face. He stared at Wally then told him, mistakenly, Neeve and Aiden had perished.

Wally cried like he'd never cried before. People tried to comfort him. He couldn't speak. Chris wandered over and thought his dad had lost it because of the fire. "It's OK, talk to me, Dad, we can get through anything now. C'mon, just talk to me!"

Wally couldn't tell him the truth, couldn't think clearly.

Eventually he forced the words from his body, Neeve and Aiden had died in the Kinglake fire.

The father and son were mute as they walked away together and got in their car. Chris dialled Bec's number and somehow got through. She answered and spoke briefly.

Wally couldn't hear what she said but suddenly Chris hurled the phone and let out a chilling scream that still comes back to haunt his father. The boy tried to get out of the car and run toward the flames, but Wally lurched across the seat grabbing at his son. He caught him by his little finger and clung on for dear, dear life.

Chris began throwing punches, not to hurt his father but just to somehow stop his own pain.

"It's Macca and Neeve. It's MACCA!" he yelled.

The mobile phone was on the floor of the car and the line was still open; Wally could hear Bec screaming in anguish.

It was at the Kinglake West CFA when Cam and Ross, a police officer and a local bloke, wept together that people got their first glimpse of the Black Saturday tragedy that was unfolding. It occurred to Cam that the rumours about the destruction of Kinglake might be true.

Realising that he couldn't get to Kinglake, Ross's focus had turned to his wife. Only his respect for Cam stopped him jumping in the car and risking his life to get down the mountain to Bec. Fortunately, one of the other police officers offered to take him to Whittlesea.

On the way, the first of a flood of welfare checks, people requesting police verify the situation of loved ones, came over the radio. So the police car, with Ross in the passenger seat, turned and headed away from Whittlesea towards Flowerdale.

The devastation along the road to Yea was apocalyptic. Houses lay in smouldering heaps; trees were still burning. It was like something Ross had only ever seen in a disaster movie. Large trees had fallen across the road; there was no way they could reach Flowerdale. Those people were on their own. Trees had also fallen to the north of Flowerdale, which meant people attempting to flee in cars had no escape route.

The police car headed back towards Whittlesea.

From the Bushfires Royal Commission

About 100 people remained in Flowerdale after the fire passed through but local CFA captain Glen Woods said no one came to check on the township.

"Flowerdale was a ghost town. We did not hear or see anyone from the outside world for three days. There were no police and the bodies were just left in situ for three days. We were still extremely busy putting out fires in the town. We had no phone communications and I could not get through on the radio channel 25."

CHAPTER 6

INTO THE CHAOS

CALLS FOR HELP and welfare checks were crackling over the CFA and police radios at Kinglake West. Cam's ears pricked up, he recognised one of the addresses in Extons Road, not far from the Kinglake football ground. It was the home of a fellow policeman and mate Matt Wheeler who worked off the mountain. Cam, Roger and the two other police officers decided it was time to try and head east, back to Kinglake.

He said goodbye to Laura and the boys with the departing words, "I'll see you soon!"

It was 7.45 p.m. on February 7.

Cam was to spend the next twenty hours in the police car.

The trip to Kinglake wasn't so much a fruitless counterattack in a battle that had already been lost, more like a sortie out into no-man's-land. Alongside the main road the smoke was still heavy and there were flames to the right and left of them. Houses and cars were burning and booming explosions vibrated their way through the car windows.

A white Holden sedan was abandoned in the westbound lane; the vehicle was blackened inside but there was no sign of the driver.

Further on they could see a major fire to their left. The Pheasant Creek general store was still ablaze and as they drew closer Cam noticed his little white ute parked up beside the building. Remarkably, it had so far avoided the flames.

They pressed on until a fallen power pole and lines blocked their path, then they had to wait for CFA and State Emergency Service crews to go to work with their chainsaws.

Cam's adrenaline was going through the roof. Ahead of them was a burned out car that looked like a Volkswagen ute. It had been towing a caravan when it collided with another car which had been heading in the other direction back towards Kinglake. Both vehicles were totally destroyed and the caravan was just a pile of ashes.

Cameron recognised the distinctive VW; it belonged to Grant Lawson who he'd worked alongside at the Gas and Fuel Corporation when he was a plumber many years earlier. There was no sign of Grant, which was partly reassuring because it meant he'd survived the crash. But all around them trees and bushes were still burning on both sides of the road.

With the sun beginning to go down and heavy smoke shrouding the mountain, it was becoming dark. Embers rained down like a million red fairy lights.

Again they drove towards Kinglake. The air conditioner in the car was on high and with the windows up tight they had a thin wall of security between themselves and the madness outside.

Horses were lying on their backs dead and bloated beside the road. Another one had survived but looked to have a broken leg.

On the right-hand side, to the south, a group of survivors huddled together near a fruit and vegetable stall. One of them had a suspected broken ankle but otherwise they said they were OK.

Cameron was beginning to try and find some logic in why some people had miraculously survived the holocaust relatively unscathed while others had perished for reasons you could only file under the heading "bad luck".

A few hundred metres further on, a huge pine tree had fallen across the road at the very instant a white Ford station wagon was travelling underneath. Incredibly, the gigantic trunk had smashed into the bonnet, missing the cabin by centimetres, and while there was fire all around them the car hadn't burned.

Cameron had to will himself through each vehicle check, worried about what he might find inside. As he got out of the police car this time near the fallen pine tree the winds were so strong he needed to steady himself to regain his footing. The winds were also fanning flames high above them in the trees and there was a risk of falling branches.

They checked the white Ford, and once more were relieved to find no one inside.

As CFA and SES (State Emergency Service) crews cut up the tree Cam discovered another group of survivors had sheltered in sheds at the nearby High Mountain Spring Water property.

A few hundred metres ahead, at the Extons Road intersection, an abandoned red Landcruiser was sitting up an embankment on a bizarre angle near the football ground. It was untouched by flames but there were still fires nearby. A time check showed 8.30 p.m.

Ross eventually made it down the smouldering and singed-red hill to Whittlesea where he found Bec. The husband and wife couldn't find the words to frame their thoughts and feelings, so they cried. Then they cried some more. When eventually the tears stopped their thoughts turned to Aiden, Calum, Mick and Jenny.

They wrongly believed both Aiden and Jenny had been badly burned. Jenny had sustained burns to almost 40% of her body while getting out of the house but Aiden was mostly unharmed. The pair of them, along with Mick, sheltered at a neighbour's home in Reserve Road before heading down to the Kinglake CFA.

Then finally some more good news. Despite a few close scrapes Calum and his mate Kevin had made it to safety at Yea. Bec and Ross found themselves on an emotional roller coaster, crying with friends, being hugged by strangers and worrying how Aiden, Jenny and Mick would get down off the mountain.

In contrast millions of Victorians were getting ready for bed that night thankful that their state had survived the hottest day on record without being burned to a cinder. They had little knowledge of the drama and horror that was unfolding within an hour's drive of the centre of Melbourne.

Some reports were starting to filter through of possible deaths but most people believed that Victorian Premier John Brumby and others, who had forewarned of the worst fire day ever, had been wrong. The Buchanans were among a small group of people who were beginning to think otherwise.

Alarmingly, no ambulances were being sent up the hill, it was deemed too dangerous, although Cameron and Roger and their crew had pushed along the main road as far as the Kinglake football ground, about five kilometres from Kinglake village.

In the meantime, the media was beginning to arrive at Whittlesea.

Cam and the small emergency services convoy turned into Extons Road near the football ground and drove past that solitary red Landcruiser sitting eerily untouched up on the embankment. On the other side of Extons Road they saw flames shooting out of the upstairs windows of the basketball stadium. The CFA crew quickly went to work.

Two other police vehicles were now with Cam and Roger; they pressed on towards Matt's place at a despairingly slow speed dodging burning branches and power poles and at times driving over fallen lines.

After about three kilometres their hearts sank. The road was just a mass of burning branches and trees for as far as they could see. They felt that they had let a good mate down but the fire was so fierce they had no option but to give up and turn around.

Back at the main road intersection the CFA crew was winning the battle to save the basketball hall so the police cars took the driveway opposite into the football ground.

Middle Kinglake Primary School was across the driveway from the oval, and it was well alight. Embers from the fire showered down on them. To their right, parked out on the oval, they could see six cars with their lights turned on and people standing about. One man asked Cameron if he could help them get some drinks and ice from the clubrooms for the kids. The Kinglake Football Netball Club president promptly kicked in the storeroom door.

The only rules they were playing by on the night of February 7 were the rules of survival.

Again on the move, they were shocked to come across a pile of grotesquely twisted and burned out vehicles which Cam figured was most likely the four-car accident they'd been called to earlier. The one he'd just missed. The one Laura had avoided because she took too long evacuating. A group of people were watching from an opposite driveway, among them Grant Lawson, whose VW had been towing the burned out caravan.

Leaning against the fence, and seemingly in pain or emotionally upset, was another of Cam's friends, Rossi, who owned the Kinglake Cappa Rossi pizza restaurant. He sponsored the football club and Cam had spent long nights eating and laughing at the restaurant and discussing life and its mysteries with Rossi's wizened father, who he knew simply as Papa. In Australian terms the elderly Italian was as nice a bloke as you'd ever wish to meet.

Rossi was repeating over and over "Papa, Papa, Papa". He told Cameron his father was in one of the vehicles. Cam's heart sank. He confirmed there was a body in Papa's car. The vehicles were still smouldering, although there were no flames. Mag wheels had melted and turned into a silver liquid that ran across the scorched and bubbled asphalt. Parts of the motors had also melted.

Cam walked back over and gently embraced Rossi, who then shocked the senior constable by asking if he'd seen his wife and four children.

They'd been in the red Landcruiser that had run up the embankment. Rossi hadn't been able to find them anywhere. Cam pulled out his mobile phone and began ringing people he knew had survived in the High Mountain sheds. Eventually one of them confirmed the five family members had made it inside and were safe and well.

Rossi collapsed into a ditch hysterical with relief. Despair and elation, but mostly despair, were constant companions that night. Roger and Cameron placed flashing lights around the wreckage then got back in the car.

The mood inside the police vehicle was sombre, they were still a kilometre from Kinglake village and already the "unimaginable" was becoming common place. They didn't know what they would find next.

Driving down the steep hill that leads into the village they felt like they were navigating through a war zone, red embers were raining down and there were flames and burning houses on both sides of the road. More blackened cars were resting against another huge pine tree that had fallen. The vehicles had been heading for the supposed safety of the township. Everywhere they looked there was chaos and destruction.

Off to one side a smaller tree had fallen and a motorbike was pinned underneath. More vehicles rested on their roofs and others had rolled down an embankment. It seemed obvious that the drivers of these vehicles couldn't see clearly enough to make the right decisions and had driven blindly into other cars.

First came the smoke, then came the fire, then came the horror.

Burned out vehicles near Kinglake village. Thick smoke cut driving visibility to zero. (Pic: Herald Sun.)

The officers had to check the cars. It was like the set of a disaster movie, except the smells and sights were real. Again Cam noticed the mag wheels and engine parts had melted. At the rear of one of the cars, still partly in the vehicle, Cam found a dog that had died in the flames.

A CFA crew was already cutting its way through the tree that blocked the road and a young man had a chain hooked up to one of the cars and was trying to tow it clear of the heap. The problem was the vehicle had been so hot it had sunk at least a centimetre into the asphalt.

Edging around the mangled mess, they were able to continue into the township where the magnitude of the catastrophe finally hit home. Where once there had been homes near the shopping centre there were now just piles of burning rubble with sparks and flames shooting into the sky. Large trees were glowing red.

Incredibly, the National Park Hotel at the top of the street was still standing. The pub was owned by Kinglake footballer Craig Lovick and partner Sharon. They thought their time had come as embers showered the historic building. People were sheltering in their cool room. Fire brigade captain Paul Hendrie evacuated those people to the CFA building, then told "Lovey" if he lost the pub it was likely the CFA shed would go with it.

Craig went outside to face the fire wearing shorts, thongs, a light top and a CFA helmet to protect his hair, which was getting singed by the embers. He and Sharon manned the hoses while locals bravely climbed onto the roof to defend the pub from that vantage point.

Across the road from the hotel a number of buildings, including the petrol station, Cappa Rossi pizza restaurant and houses had been destroyed.

Most amazing of all, and Cam couldn't believe his eyes as he drove up the main street, there were hundreds of people, perhaps as many as a thousand, wandering around apparently aimlessly. They looked to be in shock. It was like something from the *Night of the Zombies*.

One man came over to the car. Despite the horror around him Cameron had a bizarre thought: the guy looked exactly like the pop singer Leo Sayer. He had afro hair, which seemed to be giving off smoke, and his face and clothes were blackened but otherwise he appeared OK. The guy wanted to take refuge in the police station, but Cam told him that wasn't permitted.

The only lights in town glowed from the station; Cam remembered he'd set the generator going about 5.40 p.m. The building was only a few years old with big dark glass windows and doors. Visually, it remained a pillar of security and certainty in the township, but on this occasion it had been rendered useless by circumstances beyond control. The garden and veranda poles were on fire, although the building itself appeared safe.

In front of the police station a Landcruiser was also on fire. It had been towing a motor bike trailer, which was burning along with its load of three motor bikes.

At the other end of town the Cappa Rossi restaurant was gone – another blow for Rossi. Next door, the hardware store and service station, where Calum worked, was dying a spectacular death. Explosions rocked it as flames from the petrol bowsers shot metres into the night sky.

Cam couldn't imagine that in the brief history of European settlement in Australia anyone had ever witnessed scenes of such abject destruction as those unfolding in front of his eyes. Perhaps it was comparable to the Japanese bombing of Darwin.

As Roger turned the car around Cam checked his watch, it was 9.35 P.M., more than three hours since the firestorm hit Kinglake. Back at the western end of town groups of people had gathered outside the CFA building.

The two officers approached the building on foot, it seemed quiet except for the unsettling sounds of people crying and others moaning in pain. When Cameron looked inside it momentarily took his breath away; the concrete floor was covered in bodies. The victims, including Jenny Clark, were alive but in various states of distress. They were draped in silver blankets and locals were moving among the injured and burned people, attempting to help. If they were in the war zone this was surely the field hospital.

Ross and Bec Buchanan say they'll be forever grateful to Dionne Smith. She's the mother of Kevin, the young man who'd managed to escape to Yea with Calum. She has two other children, Kane and Kelsey. Kelsey was close friends with Neeve.

Bec fluked a call through to Dionne at the CFA building at 9.48 P.M., not knowing Dionne was with Jenny and Aiden. To Bec's immense relief Dionne was able to confirm that Aiden was OK. She gave Aiden the phone and he reassured his mum that he wasn't hurt but after losing his sister, a brother and an uncle the teenager was scared his father had perished as well.

"Is Dad dead?" he asked down the phone. "*Is Dad dead?*"

Bec was able to give him some good news.

Bec then desperately urged Dionne not to let Jenny die. Although the Smiths lost their own house in the fires Dionne was totally focused on helping others. The Buchanans believe if it wasn't for Dionne's support

Jenny Clark may not have survived. Over and over Dionne told Jenny she had to keep breathing. She insisted Jenny had to keep living. Her daughter now needed her more than ever. Dionne never left Jenny's side, except to check on Aiden. Mick was also with them but was fighting his own battles.

In the meantime, Trish Hendrie, Linda Craske, Robyn Pottenger and others went from person to person inside the CFA building helping and reassuring those in pain and distress.

Locals also used their own initiative to smash their way into the doctor's surgery and grab whatever supplies they could find. They then distributed the medication to those in need at the fire station. Trish had been told by her husband, local CFA captain Paul Hendrie, that no ambulances were coming. They were on their own and some patients needed urgent help.

Police and CFA people consulted among themselves and decided that a volunteer fire fighter who could barely walk and appeared to have burnt lungs would be the first person taken off the mountain. Cam, Roger and a local nurse loaded the woman into the police car and they promised to return as quickly as they could, even though they had little idea what awaited them on the road down to Whittlesea.

Trish told him they were the only emergency service vehicle they'd seen all night. It was 9.50 P.M.

As they transported their patient towards Whittlesea, Roger and Cameron were able to make it back to the Whittlesea-Yea Road intersection without incident, but they looked in disbelief at a woman standing in the middle of the road in the darkness staring at the burned forest.

"There she is, look there she is!" yelled Roger so loudly it jolted Cameron.

Her dark silhouette stood out against the immense glowing tree line behind her. The woman wasn't wearing any shoes. Roger had seen her earlier in the day in the same place and warned her to get out because the fire was on its way. Remarkably, a fire which killed over 100 people had left her untouched. However, her nearby house had been destroyed.

The police car turned south and headed downhill towards Whittlesea. All they could see in front of them were trees and power lines over the road, flames still burning and glowing embers that hit the windscreen like angry insects. Cam leaned forward and rested on the dashboard. Around them everything was red and black. He could see only ten or twenty metres in front, only as far as the headlights shone before the light disappeared in the smoke.

"Left, right, stop, slow, OK quicker." Cam navigated while Roger drove. Always in the background they could hear the laboured breathing of their patient. Her condition seemed to be worsening and at one stage Cameron thought the breathing had stopped. He was preparing mentally to resuscitate the volunteer firefighter by the burning roadside.

For a couple of seconds Cam was able to steal a glance out of Roger's window, looking west along the front of the range. As far as the eye could see the hillside was a mass of seething and flickering red. Everything was gone.

Nearing the bottom of the hill the road became clearer and they could see red and blue flashing lights in the distance. Roger tramped the accelerator and they flew past the police roadblock at warp speed. Cam could only wonder what the officers on duty were thinking as the police car emerged from the hell to their north.

Ahead illuminated signs directed them to the Whittlesea football ground, which had already been turned into a relief centre. Medical staff were waiting for them and they gratefully handed over their patient.

Cam checked the time. It was 10.40 p.m. More than five hours since he'd started work early to lend Roger a hand. During that time he thought he'd lost his family and then found them, only to fear they were all going to die together. A friend had lost two children and a brother-in-law. He'd seen bodies burned beyond recognition and his township turned into a disaster zone.

All of a sudden he felt physically and emotionally exhausted.

An elderly woman who came out of the medical centre introduced herself as Nanna and asked where they came from. They told her

Kinglake. She couldn't do enough for the two officers, washing their eyes out with water then applying oil to ease the pain.

Not for the last time the mere mention of the town Kinglake evoked a sincerely compassionate response.

Ross and Bec were still desperately worried about Jenny, and Aiden and Mick, when they saw Cameron walk out of the medical centre at Whittlesea.

As soon as he noticed them his heart tightened up. His thoughts immediately turned to Neeve, who had gone to Kinglake West Primary with Angus before transferring to Kinglake Middle. He remembered the nine-year-old as a real livewire at the football clubrooms, a radiant kid who seemed to emanate life.

Cam hugged them and felt a desperate need to help. He tried to console them. His words washed over them like water trickling over rocks. The Buchanans wanted to see their youngest son Aiden, and they wanted Jenny brought down off the mountain.

As tired as he now felt, Cameron said he was going back "up top" and would make sure they were looked after. It was easier said than done.

Some emergency service people told them to stay put in Whittlesea and get some rest. The two senior constables were having none of it and got back in a police car. They had firsthand experience of the scale of the mayhem on the mountain and knew just how desperately their local knowledge was needed.

CHAPTER 7

A NIGHT OF MAYHEM

Now heading north they had their first clear view of the extent of the devastation. As far as they could see in either direction along the face of the mountain, everything glowed red with fire. The holocaust stretched for endless kilometres. The officers were in awe of what they were witnessing, and of what awaited them.

At the bottom of the hill they could see a convoy of red and blue lights ahead of them. Their hopes rose as they counted at least twelve ambulances, five CFA tankers and a front-end loader clearing the road. They knew how desperately pleased the people would be to see some help.

It was now after 11.00 p.m.

Cam and Roger caught up with the police car at the head of the convoy. They found Terry Asquith and Scott Melville from Seymour in the lead vehicle, they couldn't hope for two better blokes or more capable officers to face the challenges that awaited them.

Cam spoke to the paramedic in the first ambulance and told him of up to 300 people at Kinglake West CFA and at least 800 at Kinglake. The guy's jaw dropped. "Shit!" A dozen ambulances weren't going to be enough.

It took about an hour to reach Kinglake West, a trip generally done in ten minutes. The ambos were keen to follow orders and press on through to Kinglake; they resisted Cam's plea to leave three units at "West". The debate swung in Cameron's favour when CFA volunteers ran across the road pleading for help, one of their mates was in a truck and badly hurt. The ambos stayed. Now Cam felt as if they were starting to make some progress; they were in a position to help people and restore some order instead of just reacting to crises.

For hundreds of metres back down the main road there was a line of red and blue flashing lights. Huge metropolitan fire trucks went past in their own convoy, and their experienced professional fire officers looked on wide-eyed at the sheer scale of the destruction and the "refugees" milling about at the CFA building.

Cam noticed people start to relax a little for the first time. Houses were still burning on both sides of the road and there were some occasional explosions, but the life-threatening stage of the emergency was finally coming to an end.

⁂

Ross and Bec lost track of time but at some stage after 11.00 p.m. they were told that a police car was bringing Jenny, Mick and Aiden down off the mountain.

Already the relief centre was taking shape at Whittlesea. Bec watched in amazement as two big containers arrived, inside were beds, medical equipment and medicines. Virtual hospital wards materialised in front of them and doctors and nurses were already beginning to treat patients.

In the distance Bec noticed a photographer leaning on a car bonnet with his zoom lens pointing directly into the wards. She told some of the men and they rushed at the cameraman screaming abuse. He was ushered out of the relief centre but was later seen trying to get back in over a fence.

To their immense relief Aiden was unhurt, at least physically, and Mick was more or less OK as well. He had a burnt nose and his eyes and throat hurt from the smoke. He had also lost his diabetic medication, but his wife was in far worse condition.

Jenny had third-degree burns to 40% of her body and was in a very bad way. She couldn't meet her daughter's gaze. Jenny looked away, crying and tearfully telling Bec that she was "sorry, so sorry".

Bec replied, "Don't you fucking die on me!"

They tried to console each other, but were inconsolable, and they tried not to think of blame, but each felt a measure of guilt over a tragedy not of their making.

Jenny was wrapped up in plastic and rushed straight to the burns unit at the Alfred Hospital. Bec went with her. Mick and Aiden headed to Cranbourne, to the south-east of Melbourne, with Bec's brother Graham.

Ross's mind was in turmoil, Cranbourne and normality seemed so far away. Cranbourne, a place where people had gone to bed thinking about a trip to the Phillip Island beaches on Sunday or regretting the extra drink they'd had as a nightcap after sweltering through the harrowing Saturday heatwave. It was only an hour and a half away on the freeways, but it was now worlds away from what the fire victims had been through.

Wally and Chris Spezza and Ross's best mate from primary school, Norm, then turned up at the Whittlesea centre. Again more hugs and consoling, plus something that was to prove immensely helpful in the weeks ahead – a "buddy" system. It was decided that no one in the Buchanan family would be left alone for a single minute. Mick Clark was also given a buddy. In their darkest moments, of which there would be many, there was always someone to reach out to.

(Buddies stayed close at hand for at least a month, or until "buddies" verged on becoming "enemies" because they were omnipresent. Mick Clark and the Buchanans eventually decided they needed more space.)

In the meantime, many people couldn't take their eyes off the fiercely spectacular red glow to the north. Ross couldn't bear to even look in that direction. Chris was also struggling. Although the Spezzas' house survived the inferno he couldn't face living there again. In the weeks ahead the home was offered to other victims and the Spezzas shifted down to the suburbs.

A generous local woman, Robyn, offered Ross and Norm beds for the night. Feeling alone inside a strange room Ross was consumed by tears before eventually drifting into an exhausted and fitful sleep at about 6.30 a.m. on Sunday morning.

※

It was nearly 12.30 a.m. when Roger and Cam arrived back at Kinglake. They left the ambulance crews to do their job at the CFA building and went across the road to the police station. The 4WD with the motor-bikes was still smouldering and flames were licking the branches of tall eucalyptus trees, which almost touched the building.

Wooden posts that held up the station veranda had burnt away at the base and the roof was resting on the downpipes. Those big dark glass windows at the front of the building, which epitomised strength and security, had been cracked by the heat. But importantly, the building survived and the generator continued to supply a steady stream of power. Inside things were just the same, although the kitchen was lit up by fires from the nearby service station. It'd been burning for hours and continued to flare into the night.

The pair grabbed a ten minute break and replenished their fluids before tackling the growing list of welfare checks. One of the checks was for a bus, possibly carrying six people, that was missing in Parkside Road. It's a no-through road and they slowly drove to the end. They couldn't find the bus, although they discovered a burned-out vehicle which had been towing a small water tanker. Eerily, there was no sign of anyone, but just metres away flames were totally engulfing a house. Roger and Cam checked it out. As they got closer they noticed that the tanker's water pump and the hoses had been destroyed. Alarm bells were going off inside their heads.

They knew that only hours earlier someone would have been

confidently preparing their mobile firefighting gear in the sanguine belief they had a good chance of protecting life and property. Then the worst firestorm in recorded Australian history arrived.

The two officers approached the house, yelling in case anybody was still around; they did a circuit of the burning building looking for signs of life. There were none.

Back in the police car they sat at the intersection where Parkside Road meets the main road and contemplated what to do next. Where to start?

They both jumped as someone banged on the car and a face appeared hard up against the window. He was covered in ash, sweat and dirt and his eyes were bulging with fear.

Cam's initial reaction was shock. After regaining his composure, he wound down the window. The guy was with a friend. They were migrant workers from the nearby broccoli farm. When the fire hit they'd run for their lives to the only safe area they could find – the middle of the broccoli patch. Although they had survived, all their possessions had been lost.

Cam sent them down to the ambos at the CFA building.

Roger then decided they should check another of the main roads into Kinglake, the one that leads to his home at St Andrews. Called the Heidelberg-Kinglake Road, it's arguably the most spectacular drive within an hour of Melbourne.

There's barely room for two cars to pass and precipitous valleys to the right-hand side on the way downhill ensure it's not a trip for the fainthearted. From the road it's impossible to see the bottom of these valleys. At least that was the case before the fires.

Since February 7 the view has become enough to set the heart racing. Black sticks, which were once trees, stand in stark grey ashen deserts and stretch hundreds of metres down into those seemingly bottomless gullies.

Roger and Cam headed south along the road not knowing what they would find. Predictably, after about two kilometres, it was impassable because of fallen trees. What was on the far side of those trees, down where the forest meets the farmland, was unknown.

That was where the firestorm had begun gathering speed for its cannonball run up the mountain.

※

The tiny hamlet of Strathewen is in the foothills, where the forest meets the farmland. It's also where fires from the north-west met with a front from the south, which was fanned by the wind change.

The Bushfires Royal Commission was told "nearly every structure in the hamlet was burnt".

※

At the police station they met up again with officers Asquith and Melville and talked about what they'd seen and what was to come. There were only the four of them. It was completely overwhelming.

A call came in about kids starting fires in the Hawkins estate, so Roger and Cam shot around there but found no one, except for a couple of people beating out spot fires with hessian bags.

They headed back along Glenburn Road; flames were starting to rise again in the trees that formed a corridor of nature reserves along both sides of the tarmac.

Not far out of the Kinglake village they came across a deserted CFA truck sitting in the middle of the road. The front windscreen was smashed and the crew was nowhere to be seen. All around them it seemed every second house was alight or already a pile of smouldering ash. The CFA truck was yet another symbol of battles fought and lost against terrible odds.

Back at the station again they enjoyed a last refreshment with Asquith and Melville before the Seymour boys hit the road. It was 2 A.M. Roger and Cam then sat watching the service station continue to burn. Some of the flames were shooting six metres into the air. They discussed their operational priorities but in complete honesty didn't know what to do next. Outside the black glass windows kilometres of chaos awaited them.

For the next hour and a half they patrolled the Kinglake streets and the main road offering help and advice. It was like trying to empty water out of a leaking boat; everywhere they looked there was destruction. They also continued to search for that missing bus carrying six people. They never found it.

Sometime after 4 A.M. the phone rang at the station. It was a senior sergeant who told Roger he needed to get home and see his family. He'd been on the job since 10 A.M. the previous day.

Roger headed off and Cam decided he needed to check in with his own family. He caught up with Laura for a coffee at Kinglake West CFA. People were anxious for any bit of news about what was happening further along the ridge. Cam told them of the immense scale of the destruction but given the extreme circumstances it seemed they'd been lucky and there were few confirmed fatalities.

In the hours ahead he was to discover the true extent of the horror.

Des Dees from Kinglake SES came up for a chat and asked Cam what happened to his own house. In the context of the night the fate of the Caine home wasn't a priority and he'd hardly given it a thought. Now it occurred to him that it was probably gone, along with so many of the memories he and Laura treasured. Laura said she and the boys had to drive through flames to get out and she was assuming the house had burned down.

Des and wife Michelle offered to follow Cam down O'Grady's Road in Pheasant Creek to do a house check. As they turned left at the smouldering ruins of the Pheasant Creek general store, Cameron was greeted by the extraordinary sight of his little white ute still standing defiantly and lonely against a blackened backdrop. Embers had burned holes in the seats and the plastic indicator lights had melted but the ute looked drivable!

Further down the road burning trees blocked their path, forcing them to drive up along embankments. Fortunately, the trees had fallen after Laura and the boys had escaped. The little gully that brought tranquillity to the Caine world was glowing red, but through the branches he caught a glimpse of their home. Their front fence and nearby trees were alight, but the house was still standing!

Cam ran to the rear of the house. No damage! Around the side of the house, which was closest to the flames, the garden furniture and laser light roofing had melted. Fire had burned up to and around the wooden veranda posts.

He smiled and sighed with relief. *How freakin' lucky are we!* he thought.

Des and Michelle told him that every house they'd visited since the firestorm had been destroyed.

Later he and Laura were to spend sleepless nights thinking of those who weren't so "freakin' lucky". And then when that all became too much they would cry together. Survivor guilt, they call it. The Caines had it in spades. So many friends had lost homes, many had lost loved ones.

Night after night when Cam and Laura went to bed those same thoughts came back to trouble them. It was impossible to rationalise. Their house, nestled in a gully and surrounded by vegetation, survived, while people who had every right to expect their property would be safe lost everything, including their lives. Eventually Laura told her husband she believed they'd come through the disaster relatively unscathed so they could help others.

For every story of a miraculous escape the ledger was balanced by a tale of desperately sad misfortune. Misfortune? Misfortune doesn't quite do it.

Ross's children died in the safest house in a semi-suburban street. The Buchanan house, on the edge of the national park, survived even though flames billowed from the tree line along the rear boundary.

When Ross eventually returned home the panel van was sitting where he left it with ash on the front seat. "But what about the cat, Ross?"

"Yes, the fucking cat survived."

Not far from the Buchanan house a brick home had burned to the ground, while next to it stood a highly flammable fibreglass boat. How can that be?

Of course there's a rational and scientific answer for every single thing that burnt, or didn't burn, on February 7. But that wouldn't stop many from thinking that God owed them some answers about His unfathomable choices.

Cam, Des and Michelle went next door to check on the neighbour's home. It too had survived. The front yard was alight and flames were slowly burning towards the house nearly twelve hours after the front had swept through. They extinguished the fire without too much difficulty. Des and Michelle then drove off to check on more friends while Cam returned to Kinglake West.

He embraced Laura and told her the good news. Tears of relief followed. Harry and Angus were sound asleep on the concrete floor. Cameron bent over and gently kissed them goodnight. It was nearly 6 A.M. on Sunday morning. He wouldn't see his family again for another fifteen life-changing hours.

∽

On his own, and on his way back to Kinglake in the police car, Cameron had time to ponder what he knew.

The radio was carrying stories about bushfires in many parts of the state. There was concern for the town of Marysville, which had borne the brunt of that Murrindindi fire, and they'd also copped it in Gippsland, Bendigo (provincial Bendigo for heaven's sake!) and elsewhere.

Casualties were uncertain but it was possible many people were dead. That was unthinkable, but not impossible given what he'd seen so far. ABC Radio had reported prior to midnight that up to fourteen people were feared dead in the fires, with six perishing in Kinglake alone. Eventually the overall death toll would reach 173.

Cam was at the epicentre. He felt very much alone and the truth was he didn't know what to do.

He went back to the four-car pile-up on top of the mountain. A lone person was standing there wrapped in a blanket. It was Vicky Lacey. She was simply waiting around so no one else would plough into the cars.

The woman in the blanket and the four-car pile-up

Vicky Lacey had been at the Whittlesea music festival with her eighteen-year-old daughter when they noticed smoke in the distance from the Kilmore East fire and decided to head home.

She drove a number of times between her partner's house in Kinglake West and her own home in Kinglake to check things were OK. She was worried about her animals, particularly her favourite mare.

By late in the day a water tanker had been placed across the main road near Kinglake West CFA to stop cars heading towards Whittlesea. Senior Constable Roger Wood was concerned about the fire on the Whittlesea-Yea Road and he told Vicky and others to head back towards Kinglake.

Behind them to the west, Vicky could see flames that looked to be soaring at least ten metres into the air. She knew it was time to get away with her three teenage children.

At some stage she must have driven past Cameron Caine in his little white ute heading in the other direction towards Kinglake West, but she doesn't recall seeing him. However, Vicky remembers clearly there was no smoke at the top of National Park Road and none at the footy ground, but further on closer to Kinglake village it was turning black.

Before she knew it the smoke turned day into night and she slammed into the rear of another vehicle, which was stopped in the middle of the main road. Vicky could just make out a tangled mess of cars in front of her; she had smashed into vehicle number four, and she knew the fire was coming.

A friend called Gibbo was slumped in number four; he was barely moving and looked like he'd given up. Behind her she noticed a man crawling along the road on his hands and knees. He'd been trapped in one of the other cars but the force of the latest collision had jolted him free.

Vicky and her children moved quickly to pull Gibbo out of his car. Rossi then narrowly missed ramming them all.

With some help from the others she managed to reverse her badly damaged car away from the wreckage and drove slowly to an adjacent paddock where Rossi also parked.

Although it was dark Vicky could tell there was fire coming at them from two directions. Six people were crammed inside her car with blankets covering them.

The fire hit them with a force she'd never experienced before. It roared over the top of them with such astounding energy it made the car rock violently. It sounded as if someone was spraying their vehicle with stones, but the stones were glowing embers. Vicky was sure the car's LPG tank would explode, incinerating them all.

Soon it was so hot inside they couldn't breathe; they had to take a risk and open a door. The scorching air filled the car but provided little relief. Through the open door Vicky got a glimpse of a kangaroo and a wallaby hopelessly trying to find shelter between the two vehicles.

She was so desperately scared for the safety of her children that she doesn't recall how long she stayed in the car, it may have been half an hour, it may have been twice that long.

As the smoke began to clear they climbed out into the blackened paddock. Explosions rocked the burning cars nearby on the main road. Rossi was screaming "Papa is in that!" but no one went close to the red-hot wreckage.

Further up the hill another vehicle was on fire outside a church, which was in the process of burning to the ground. All around them was utter chaos. People emerged from the grassy areas underneath the huge electricity transmission towers; two of them had survived by sheltering in a pipe.

One of Vicky's friends, Bill, pulled up in a car with his arms badly burned. Another man had been torched from head to toe, they sat him in an armchair outside a house, which had somehow survived the inferno, and sprayed water on him. No one touched him. When he needed to be moved they carried the armchair.

Back at the crash site more cars were coming to grief as they travelled along the main road. Their drivers were looking for loved ones or looking to find out where the long trail of disaster ended and where they could find safety. Vicky and others located torches and began waving them at the traffic, then they noticed a man who seemed to appear out of nowhere and was taking pictures of the wreckage.

He mumbled something about the "coroner's office" then told them there was a body in the back seat of one of the cars. Rossi, fearing it was his father, collapsed as Cameron Caine and Roger Wood arrived.

Vicky remained at the crash site, on and off, for hours while her children joined nearly thirty other people sheltering at the nearby house. The kids, some just toddlers, refused to sleep inside because they were scared the house might catch fire. They huddled together on blankets outside as more explosions reverberated through the pungent Kinglake night air.

Vicky found out later that her own house, and all the animals, had survived the conflagration. However, her white horse was missing for days. She eventually heard that a guy had nearly hit the mare as he sped from the fires. When he swerved and slowed down the horse began to follow him. It trailed him all the way through the bedlam until he reached his house, then it stood leaning against another car, badly injured and completely spent.

When Vicky finally tracked down her beloved mare a woman had covered it with a wet blanket to help the burns. The horse's mane was singed and the tail had been burned off. One of its rear hooves was pointing inwards because of a dislocated hip, and the mare also seemed to be blind. Vicky was distraught. Eventually she was able to find a vet to help save the mare. He said it was too late; the horse had to be put down.

Bec sobbed and cried most of the way to the Alfred Hospital where her mother was to have surgery. Her mind wouldn't accept that her children were gone. She couldn't begin to imagine a life without them, that they were "no more".

For as long as she could remember she had wanted to be a mum. Work and a caree had always been a distant second. Just thinking about that phone call she received from Jenny saying "the kids are gone" sent a bolt of negative energy through her mind. It was only a memory but it had a visceral impact on her. It still does.

At the hospital Jenny was rushed away to Emergency while a nurse put an arm around Bec and walked her down the corridor. "Are you OK?" she asked.

Bec told her about the deaths. The nurse stopped in her tracks and then guided Bec to a private waiting room where they checked on her every fifteen minutes to make sure she didn't harm herself.

She wanted to make some calls but Calum's phone was running low on battery and of course she didn't have the charger. Shit! Bec borrowed a hospital phone and rang her sister-in-law, Gabe, to try and make some sense of what she was going through. Of course there was no sense to be made of it. This was to be the first of many crying and screaming sessions she would have. As she sat there exhausted and emotionally overwrought, for the first time in her life Bec had an out-of-body experience.

She had heard other people talk about the weird phenomenon of observing yourself from outside the body but now she was able to look from a distance at the shell of Rebecca Buchanan.

The shell felt as if it could easily be crushed by the weight of the grief bearing down on her. She felt as if she could die, right there in the hospital. But of course, she didn't.

She drifted in and out of sleep until a nurse fetched her to accompany Jenny on the trip from Emergency to Ward Six. It was about 5.00 a.m.

Her mother lay on the bed staring vacantly. There was no communication. Nurses gave Bec a pillow and a blanket and she curled up in a chair to grab some sleep, but a proper sleep was something that belonged to a previous life.

Cameron Caine was by himself in the police car. He drove to the Kinglake CFA building to see if there was anything else he could do. Maybe he could follow-up some missing person queries.

Two sergeants he didn't recognise were standing near the ambulances. He was relieved to have some backup, but they quickly put those hopes to rest. They'd been ordered to accompany the ambos on their trip back down the mountain.

All too soon he was on his own again, except for the thousand or so numb bushfire survivors. Fortunately, he was at ease with his local friends as he moved among them talking and consoling. He noticed that while the roar of the fire was gone it'd been replaced by the sobs of the traumatised.

From the main street people could still hear houses burning and the occasional explosion. At the eastern end of town the service station was alight more than twelve hours after the fire swept through and was continuing to throw a dramatic geyser of flame into the early morning sky.

It was nearly 7 A.M. Daylight had broken and Cameron wasn't certain if he wanted to see what the sun was about to reveal.

Kinglake's petrol station, about 100 metres from the police building. (Pic: Police Life.*)*

CHAPTER 8

MY TOWN IS GONE

KINGLAKE CFA CAPTAIN Paul Hendrie asked Cam if he'd help check some friends' homes in Ward Street. They drove slowly along backstreets. The whole nightmarish landscape was a smouldering black lightly dusted with grey. More light-as-talcum grey ash swirled in the air like a July fog on the mountain.

As he got out of the car the grey ash came nearly to the top of his police boots. It was still hot. He could feel the heat through the leather.

It was quiet, deathly quiet. The silence was only broken now and again by a falling tree branch, which seemed to echo up and down the valleys for kilometres.

They surveyed ground zero.

Sheets of scorched metal in the driveways that used to be cars, here and there a lone chimney, piles of rubble that were once houses or sheds. There was also something else that was to be with them for weeks: the near nauseating stench of smoke and burnt remains.

For a few minutes they wandered around calling out for people, humans reaching out hopefully for each other in the face of outrageously long odds. Nothing could have survived this holocaust. Nothing did survive it. They couldn't speak or even look at each other. It was time to go.

Now the tragedy was taking on a different perspective. Much of the immediate urgency had gone out of the situation but sunrise was casting a new light on the magnitude of the disaster.

Once more he drove back towards Kinglake West. A lone police officer coping with the nuclear-like destruction of his town. He remembered back to when he joined the police force, how he thought he'd welcome some real action. But this was beyond real, it was surreal. Not a whimsical Dali type of surreal, more something sinister and hellish like Dante's *Inferno*.

Houses were gone. Hundreds of them burned to the ground. The national park was gone as far as he could see towards Yarra Glen and back in the other direction to Whittlesea. He felt that now familiar tightening in the chest again. The former plumber is not given to melodrama but he came up on the police radio to D24 in Wangaratta and said, "Kinglake is gone, my town is gone". He couldn't speak anymore without becoming too emotional and he wouldn't risk that with so many other officers listening in.

The outside world was getting its first real insight into Black Saturday.

Ross spent two hours in the bedroom of a Whittlesea house alone with black thoughts that kept bouncing back into his mind like a ball on an elastic string. He would try to think of something different, try to think good thoughts about the loved ones who had survived the holocaust but always the heartache would return in milliseconds. This dragged on into minutes and then restless hours until he was relieved that it was 8.30 A.M. and time to get up and find Bec.

At the Alfred Hospital Bec felt she was going into emotional free fall and called Dionne, who immediately said she was coming in. She brought Calum with her. Bec still hadn't seen her eldest son and she badly needed to be there for him. She held Calum as if it was the last hug she would ever have.

Then, over the following hours, more family and friends arrived. They were in a state of shock. By midday on Sunday February 8 media reports were warning that dozens of people were dead, Kinglake had been destroyed and the town of Marysville was virtually razed from the face of the Earth.

The visitors were all willing Jenny to live and offering Ross and Bec fresh shoulders to cry on.

There were also some minor snippets of good news. Danny's beloved dog Bear somehow survived the fires. He'd been seen in the background of TV footage running down Reserve Road! Meanwhile, the Buchanans' dog Jazz had turned up at the Kinglake CFA. Both dogs had suffered smoke inhalation and Bear had burned paws but amazingly they'd cheated the odds.

Other friends called to wish Ross well and tell him that they'd already begun gathering supplies at Whittlesea to take back up the mountain.

Every so often Cameron would stop the patrol car and wind down the window. There was absolute silence except for the ringing in his ears. It was like the day after the end of the world.

Dead native animals and livestock lined the roadside and were scattered across the paddocks. Back up near the four-car collision Cam noticed a familiar vehicle coming towards him. It was his sergeant, Jon Ellks, arriving for work.

Cam looked exhausted. He was exhausted. It was 8.30 a.m. and he'd been on the job for fifteen hours through a night of unspeakable trauma.

Jon asked, "What's gone on?"

Cam's honest answer was "I don't know."

But he did know something about the four-car pile-up. He nodded at it and said, "Papa is in there."

Jon walked quickly towards the tangle of burnt metal, took a look and then turned in horror. "Let's get back to the station."

Over a cup of coffee Cameron filled his sergeant in as best he could on the horrific events he'd seen since the night before. The briefing was punctuated by repeated police radio calls from D24 in Wangaratta for welfare checks.

The phone was also starting to ring off the hook. As the list kept growing they just looked at each other. Where to start? Outside in the main street of Kinglake small groups of people were being reunited with friends and family. They were hugging and crying in each other's arms.

One of the calls for a welfare check was on the Clarks' house in Reserve Road. Cam's heart sank, it was a job he didn't want to do but a job he'd signed up for ten years earlier when he gave up plumbing and joined the Victoria Police.

Another officer from Seymour, Matt McPartlan, arrived. Sergeant Ellks left McPartlan in charge of the station while they went out on the first of a seemingly inexhaustible list of welfare checks, including Number One Reserve Road.

Cam's sense of foreboding grew as they made the short drive to purgatory. Cars had slammed into each other and burned on the eastern edge of town just as they had on the western entrance to Kinglake. Most of the houses had been destroyed and again there was this ubiquitous deathly silence.

Cameron walked around the perimeter of where the Clarks' Reserve Road house had once stood and then approached the pile of rubble. Nearing where the rear of the house had been, the house where five people had perished, his worst fears were confirmed. He stepped backwards in shock.

Cam retreated and slumped down on the garden path, taking short shallow breaths as if someone had thrown a bucket of cold water on him. Sergeant Ellks wanted to know if he was OK, and while Cam answered yes, deep inside he was gutted. The senior constable knew he couldn't panic or lose it. He had plenty of other places on the list to visit.

Months later Bec wanted to know more about what Cameron had

seen. He told her the truth, and thankfully, it was the news she wanted to hear. The children and Danny were together in their final moments.

Slowly he walked to the front of the property and sealed it off with tape.

Cameron then sat alone in the police car trying once more to make sense of what had just confronted him. Then Sergeant Ellks rejoined him and they checked two more addresses. They found six more victims including an entire family of four he knew through Auskick, the children's football clinics, at the Kinglake club.

They then went back to the four-car pile-up and taped it off again. It was 10.30 A.M.

At the other end of the ridge Cam and Sergeant Ellks checked Ryans Road, Pine Ridge Road and National Park Road. They were shocked at the devastation. Ross later counted just fourteen houses still standing in National Park Road while ninety-six were in ruins.

Many of Cam's friends from the football and netball club lived in this area where lots of houses were built close together. For these folks it was only five minutes to the Whittlesea-Yea Road and then a quick trip down the mountain and into the suburbs or city for work.

Cameron noted that Ross and Bec's house had survived, so had Wally's next door and the Barlows' home across the road. But civilisation in Pine Ridge Road at the end of National Park Road was obliterated. Two days after Cam and Jon went through the streets the remains of nine people were discovered in a small room in one burned out house.

Where once there were houses and gardens and kids' bikes and pets, now there was nothing, save for the omnipresent grey ash.

The two police officers continued searching through houses and swimming pools. Each time he came to a pool Cam slowly moved the covers back, desperately hoping there would be no one under them.

Back at the station just before midday Scott and Terry from Seymour met up with them after grabbing a few hours' sleep. That meant Sergeant Ellks was able to split the welfare checks into two groups, and the local officers certainly needed the help, with ten calls alone coming in just after 12.30 p.m.

An inspector also arrived and by chance Cam was related to him – Tom McGillian had married one of Cameron's cousins. The inspector had an air of incredulity about him after driving through the utter destruction on the way up from Whittlesea. Tom asked what the local crew needed.

Cam said, "Diesel for the generator and smokes."

He allowed himself a brief smile, the only one since he'd kissed the kids goodbye sometime in the early hours at Kinglake West CFA. Cam was on a give-up-smoking campaign and had been taking tablets for a fortnight. He'd set Sunday February 8 as the day he was finally going to quit. Now, he re-set his quit date to sometime in the future.

Over the next three hours they continued checking addresses. The list of fatalities grew; however, the list of friends and others who were unaccounted for got smaller. Cam was still running on adrenaline but starting to feel very tired. He had to think hard to remember when he'd last eaten.

At 3.00 p.m. Cameron received his final call for help. A guy in need of medical attention was unable to get out of his own property. Cam and Sergeant Ellks drove through paddocks to collect him and then dropped the man with the paramedics. By now they were low on fuel and because the servo in Kinglake had been destroyed, they had to drive thirty-one kilometres to Whittlesea just to fill up.

Each time Cam had driven up or down the main road he was overwhelmed by the extent of the damage. It was literally breathtaking. His world was awash in black and grey, the all-pervading post-disaster colour scheme. Occasionally there were little pockets of green, the colour of life. The green looked so out of place, but so attractive to the eye. Green was the most beautiful colour in the world.

In Whittlesea itself the road to the mountain was now well and truly blocked off, but there were people and emergency vehicles everywhere. As well as the football oval, the cricket ground near the secondary college was also bursting with vans and trucks. Cameron wasn't comfortable around the relief facilities. While he could see emergency workers were doing an essential job, he felt he was most needed at the centre of the disaster, with his own people.

Back up top again the two police officers stopped at the ruins of the Pheasant Creek general store. Cameron climbed into his little white ute and turned over the motor. All the plastic externals closest to the fire had melted but the ute started like clockwork! It was freakish.

Cam's ute survived the burnover and started without a problem. (Pic: Police Life.)

They drove both vehicles back to the police station. It was 4.40 P.M. on Sunday and Cam was mentally and physically spent. His eyes were still burning from the smoke and his joints ached.

Roger Wood walked in to start his shift. "You still here?" he said. He was followed by the local inspector and a senior sergeant. They sat around for a de-briefing and Cam told them he'd had enough. He was going home. It was nearly twenty-four hours since he'd started work early to help Senior Constable Wood and seen a flickering light through the trees.

For the record

Along the Pentadeen Spur in Kilmore East the power cable stretches for a kilometre between two poles, known as pole 38 and pole 39. It's one of the longest sections of electricity line in Victoria and was built in 1966.

The Bushfires Royal Commission heard that on pole 39 the helical termination, where the power cable is held in place, hadn't been fitted properly.

The device resembles the rounded end of a pulley where the cable clips in place between the rims of the wheel. As it was put to the Bushfires Royal Commission, the cable is supposed to "lock on to the conductor". But someone had erred. The cable wasn't locked on and instead ran across the top of the device and was hard up against a metal pin. That meant there was less give and more strain on the cable.

An expert who had inspected tens of thousands of power poles told the Royal Commission he'd seen this happen on only three occasions.

It's not known which linesman made the initial error with the placement of the cable or why his judgement was so clouded on that particular day. Maybe it was late in the afternoon and he was thinking about knocking off? Perhaps his mind was on the football or his partner or hurrying home for a cold beer.

It's alleged that the extra strain on the cable, and the constant winds, weakened it to such an extent that on February 7 it snapped and then whipped back and struck the stay on pole 38. This, it's claimed, sent superheated plasma gas into the dry grass below.

It may have been just a cupful of plasma but at 5,000 degrees it's alleged it was sufficient to start a fire on a farm belonging to John Stewart.

The northerly winds then pushed it into a pine plantation.

Within hours 119 people were dead.

The company responsible for the power line has rejected this explanation and claims the line was actually brought down by a lightning bolt.

Senior Constables Caine (left) and Wood revisit scenes of devastation days after the tragedy. (Pic: Police Life.*)*

CHAPTER 9

THE FREIGHT TRAINS COMETH

THE LIGHTS WERE out in the bedroom, but Cam's brain was firing like a pinball machine. He'd travelled to Whittlesea about 8.00 p.m. on Sunday to be reunited with his family, who were staying at his cousin's house.

Tom McGillian was the first to notice Cam had arrived but soon Laura emerged and ran to the edge of the veranda where they hugged like he'd been away for years. Angus and Harry weren't far behind. Sian was still with friends.

Laura had been trying to call all day. She said things were still so chaotic up on the mountain she wasn't sure if he was alive or dead.

Bec and Ross had also been calling; they wanted the closure that Cam couldn't give them. Bec wanted to know, needed desperately to know, if the children had died together, or were they perhaps caught while trying to flee the property? But the deaths of the children were now in the hands of the coroner. Cam was 100% certain he'd seen the bodies of Neeve and Macca but he was praying he'd made a mistake and that somehow, inexplicably, they had survived.

He couldn't tell Bec and Ross.

Cam had a long shower and something to eat then shuffled off to bed completely exhausted. He turned off the lights and thought about the people at Kinglake who still needed him. There was so much to do.

Then it happened. It felt like freight trains were rushing through his brain.

Wild and disturbing recollections of the devastation he'd seen in the past thirty hours flashed by. They wouldn't stop. They took him back inside the homes where he'd seen things he couldn't talk about and then back outside again running from the fire.

Jesus. What's going on? His mind was racing out of control. He steadied and listened to his own laboured breathing then another batch of distressing images arrived.

At some stage tormented sleep eventually found him.

*

Late on the Monday afternoon following the fires Cam, Laura and the boys headed home for the first time. They inspected the house together; a rear door had been blackened, part of the deck roof had melted, there were scorch marks on the carpet in the rumpus room and the pump wiring was a mass of congealed copper and plastic.

There was no power, the water tank was polluted and the house stank of smoke. But at least it was still a house, their house, and for that they were grateful.

They went back to the police station for a shower. The building was full of officers from downtown. They couldn't do enough for Laura and the kids. In fact later in the week some coppers from Footscray chipped in and hired the Caines a generator. They took Cameron out the back of the station and handed the "gennie" over, telling him to keep it for as long as he wanted.

The senior constable was short on words as he tried to express his gratitude.

On the Monday night they slept at Cameron's parents' house. As Cam drifted off to sleep the freight trains started to arrive again, but this time he could actually see the carriages in his dream. A freight train was rushing through a crowded fiery street. People were running everywhere amid the flames! The intensity of the noise was almost unbearable. Cam could feel the heat, see the faces, smell the smoke. It was so real and so disturbing it woke him up.

Sweat was running down his face. He stared at the ceiling.

Slowly, with foreboding in his heart, he looked over at Laura. She seemed to be dead.

Cam thought he was sleeping beside a corpse.

He was certain it was one of the corpses he'd seen the day before.

Cam rubbed his eyes. He felt edgy and hotwired. He couldn't bring himself to look at his wife again and sat up in bed.

Laura sensed the movement and woke up. Oh God! He'd been dreaming or hallucinating or… he didn't know what the hell he'd been doing. He was at a loss to explain it. Worse was to come.

CHAPTER 10

ROSS TACKLES THE MEDIA

Ross also headed home on the Monday, or at least he tried to.

After visiting Jenny and Bec in hospital he drove to Whittlesea, where the relief centre had become, in his words, a media circus.

All of Australia wanted to learn more about what was shaping up as the worst natural disaster in the nation's history. The speed and destruction of the bushfires had been a phenomenon of unprecedented proportions. Now another phenomenon was underway.

Dismayed at the footage, photos and stories emanating from the bushfire zones, Australians were beginning to respond with offers of cash, food or anything else that could be of use to the survivors. Weeks later they were still giving, with the bushfire appeal topping an extraordinary $386,000,000! Or nearly $20 from every man, woman and child in Australia.

The closed shop nature of Australian TV, which is dominated by four free-to-air national networks, helped unite the country in a common cause.

But survivors on the frontline paid a price as their privacy, and what could be salvaged from their pre-Black Saturday lifestyle, was sacrificed on the altar of media demands. At first Ross was incensed by the sheer idiocy of the "how do you feel?" question which the reporters put to him and other survivors. He wanted to tell the reporters the truth, tell them that he felt like a piece of him had died too. Or that he felt like his heart had been removed while he was still conscious. But instead he just politely mumbled that everyone was doing the best they could under the circumstances.

Soon he realised that his answers were the words that accompanied the stunning pictures, which in turn enticed Australians to dip into the story and their pockets. The sheer magnitude of the generosity took everyone by surprise.

But Ross was also shocked at the way the media machine sometimes packaged the story. While he was at the Whittlesea Relief Centre he was hugged by one of Macca's fifteen-year-old friends in what was a private moment of grief sharing.

Hungry for emotive images of distress or relief the cameras swamped the pair as they embraced. Ross later heard that the footage was seen around the world. The first time he saw it was during a Sony promo for a fundraiser CD, which went to air late at night wedged in between two advertisements for phone sex.

Ross felt his mourning of the death of his children was something pure, sacrosanct and personal; it was upsetting to see it turned into a marketing tool and placed alongside titillating advertisements that targeted the raincoat brigade.

Then there were the front-page pictures to cope with. Bec released photos of Neeve, Macca and Danny to the newspapers. She doesn't know to this day how the Herald Sun newspaper found her phone number, but the children's mother wanted to choose which photos were displayed to the public, as well as ensure all the details were correct.

Those pictures were networked around the world, and Bec began receiving international letters of condolence, including one from England that was addressed "Rebecca Buchanan, Somewhere in Kinglake". A £20 note was inside.

Although she green-lighted the publication of the pics it was still a strange sensation to see the children's images in the public domain. It was as if they'd become public property and everyone in Australia, perhaps the world, had a share in the ownership of the memories of Neeve and Macca.

Ross wasn't completely at ease with the decision to release the photos, especially when the children were named in the media prior to the coroner confirming the deaths. His media angst would have been worse if he knew what was taking place at his own house while he was off the mountain. Reporters had quickly figured out where the parents of the dead children lived and were camped outside waiting to interview friends or relatives.

Wally confronted the journalists and camera crews and told them to get off the property. Other locals labelled them ghouls. But they were simply conduits for the stories that all of Australia wanted to learn more about.

The whole country was mourning the deaths of Macca and Neeve and all the others who perished, and they wanted to know more about the personalities behind those desperately sad photos which hinted at much but revealed so little.

While the media may have had early and easy access to the fire zone, it was tougher for locals to get "back up top". This caused some resentment, and from resentment stems anger. People stranded off the mountain all had friends and family in the fire zone who were short of food, particularly perishables.

Ross and three mates, Norm, Todd and Vin, filled a truck with supplies and headed north out of Whittlesea on the Monday. They were stopped at the first police roadblock and sent back. It took hours to organise passes.

Other Kinglakers regaled Cam with similar stories when he arrived at Whittlesea. Five cars carrying locals gathered outside the home of Kinglake netball coach Cat Muir and her partner, Kinglake footballer Jarrod Heal. They wanted Cam to help them "get home". Together they drove to the Whittlesea Foodworks supermarket to stock up.

When Cameron explained he was a Kinglake police officer and they needed to take badly needed groceries into the disaster area the manager told them to "grab what you want".

He couldn't do enough to help them. They cleaned him out of bread and stocked up on tea, coffee, biscuits, ice, milk, smokes, clean underwear, feminine hygiene products and anything and everything people had been phoning and asking for.

Emerging from the supermarket, Cam was confronted by a growing problem. He'd been recognised by other Kinglakers. People at the far end of the main street were calling out his name, soon more were converging and his first impulse was to hide. It was overwhelming; he could barely cope with the group of close friends he'd met earlier let alone an extra dozen or so asking for help.

Cameron knew precisely what everyone wanted. They were about to implore him, their local copper, to get them through or around the police roadblocks.

The senior constable agreed to give it a try. He told them all to meet in Milky Lane, so they would avoid the first roadblock, and then to cram into as few vehicles as possible before they arrived at the second police obstacle.

Seven cars, crowded with passengers and groceries, converged on the roadblock at the foot of the mountain.

From the Bushfires Royal Commission

Evidence was heard that police on site could use their own initiative to impose a total roadblock. However, they were not empowered to then downgrade a total roadblock to a partial roadblock without the consent of the incident controller.

But even when there was a total roadblock in place it seemed there were exceptions.

Counsel Assisting –

"… So when there is a fire approaching, during that fire and in the immediate aftermath of the fire… members of the police working with the guidelines have no discretion to allow through people delivering supplies to those behind the roadblock?"

Police Assistant Commissioner Kieran Walshe –

"Look, I think the guidelines do allow some discretion but you can't be in a situation that if somebody is coming with relief it's necessary to prevent them entering… the guidelines are there but they should never take away the discretion of a member of Victoria Police to act in a situation where it is quite proper to allow access for a specific purpose."

Victoria Police has moved to clarify the roadblock policy, with the emphasis now on "compassion and common sense."

Cam approached the roadblock outside Whittlesea and explained to the officers who he was and what they were carrying. Perhaps the police figured that if the seven-car convoy was allowed through the first roadblock then there was no need to stop them heading up the hill. They got the nod from the officers.

They drove up to Kinglake West and along the ridge. For Cameron it was a now familiar trip through a landscape from hell. For others in the convoy their journey home left them jaw agape. Burnt cars littered the roadside. Everywhere they looked familiar houses and landmarks had been transformed into ashen ruins. Stumps and fallen trees were giving off smoke and occasionally a small flame flickered.

In Kinglake township it was hot and dusty with strong winds blowing ash down the main street. Locals who'd spent the night fighting fires further to the north, or blacking out hot spots on their own properties, looked like they'd been rolling in charcoal. CFA trucks and water tankers lined the road.

On the south side of the street buildings had been destroyed at both ends of town. Burnt cars bore testimony to the speed of the fire, and the helplessness of those who were trapped with nowhere left to flee.

Cam spotted a new 4WD vehicle cruising through town. One door was missing, and in a cursory nod to safety a rope had been tied in place to prevent the driver sliding out when he took corners.

Ambulances and police cars cluttered the street and everywhere people were busily trying to establish a foothold on their former lives. Occasionally a CFA truck, with lights flashing and sirens blaring, would speed off and only then would the activity stop and silence return to the township for a brief few seconds.

Welcome to the war zone.

Among the chaos Cam met Victoria's police chief commissioner, Christine Nixon, who told him she'd heard a lot about him. Although police hadn't been ordered to evacuate people during the fires, Senior Constable Caine and some other officers had used their initiative to save lives whenever the opportunity arose.

Bushfires Royal Commission, Assistant Commissioner Kieran Walshe

A/C Walshe told the hearing he was unaware of police being advised by any controlling agency at any stage on February 7 to warn the public about the approaching dangers of the fires, nor was he aware of police receiving any call to evacuate people.

However, he alluded to a number of incidents when police used their own initiative to evacuate people –

"Constable Caine got out of the police car and stayed at the

[Pheasant Creek] general store on foot whilst Senior Constable Wood headed up to Kinglake West to ensure it was clear and Constable Caine [then] sent all the vehicles back up along the road... then he got in the last vehicle... as he went away he did notice that fire came across the road and that the general store was destroyed."

Also –

"Police became aware of a number of people on the oval... at Marysville. They were aware, the police were aware, of the fire's imminent presence; they could see it quite clearly. They went there and after Leading Senior Constable Hamill had been to the CFA for advice as to which way to go he'd gone down to the oval with some other police and there were about 200 people there with cars and caravans... and with the assistance of other people, the CFA et cetera led them out of town and to Buxton [safely]."

A/C Walshe also cited other examples at Kilmore East and Strathewen.

"It was like something out of Ethiopia."

Those were Cameron's first thoughts as he stood outside the CFA building and watched a long convoy bringing supplies into town. Where the convoy came to a halt there was bickering, tension and even some anger over whose job it was to consign the aid.

The Red Cross had arrived in town. They had their own organisational structures, but so did the locals who believed they'd been coping well up until Monday afternoon and had firsthand knowledge of where the priorities should be.

Although he wasn't wearing his uniform Cam sensed that frustrations could boil over, and that shouting matches had the potential to degenerate into "push and shove". He produced his police badge and urged people to "calm down". They then decided to send a lot of the aid back to Kinglake West.

Another Kinglake footballer, Gav Hodgson, offered to use his house as a storeroom for the goods that were rolling into town. Soon his rooms were stacked floor to ceiling.

The aid process was getting some structure to it and Cameron marvelled at the avalanche of food, bedding, clothing and other items arriving in Kinglake. They were at the pointy end of an Australia-wide charity campaign that was just gaining momentum.

He and many other Kinglakers from that day on felt very proud of their fellow Australians and the country they were a part of.

Soon Australian flags started to spontaneously appear on many of the burnt properties. It's unclear whether the sentiment behind the flag phenomenon was a feeling that the "Aussie spirit stands resolute" or something less assertive, perhaps "we're all in this together". Unlike Americans, Aussies are generally not flag flyers and overt patriots.

Back in National Park Road Ross Buchanan was transfixed by the sight of a solitary clothesline still strung with kids' tops and pants but surrounded by a scene of ashen annihilation. Remarkably, his woodpile and his shed had burned but the house remained. He entered through the front door and went back into another world, a pre-fires world.

Neeve's clothes were laid out in preparation for her trip to the Whittlesea Music Festival on Saturday night. Ross couldn't bring himself to touch them and his mate Vin put the little girl's clothes away for the last time.

The Buchanan property in National Park Road. Remarkably the house was still standing but the backyard and Ross's pumps were destroyed. (Pic: family collection.)

In the meantime, Wally had told Ross about the reporters who had to be kicked off the front lawn. Ross also noticed the journalists were dressed similarly to CFA volunteers which, he believed, gave them easy access to the Kinglake ridge. He was becoming angry.

More correctly, he was already angry and he just got madder. He was looking for someone to unload his frustrations on and the media were shaping up as a worthy punching bag.

Locals could only move around under tight travel restrictions but the media seemed to have the run of the town. Ross had never locked his house, but decided things had changed and he simply couldn't trust the journos not to go inside.

TV, radio and newspaper reports may have turned a trickle of relief supplies into a flood of bushfire assistance but as far as the locals were concerned it came at an ever-steepening price.

Back outside Ross noticed that an Australian flag was still flying over the blackened property of neighbour Daniel "Doggy" Heal. Doggy's brick house was gone but the flagpole and a little patch of green grass had survived. He told Ross the flag would stay at half-mast until Macca and Neeve's funerals were over.

It was just the inspiration Ross needed to tackle the media. The simmering anger boiled over and he got in a car and headed back down to the media circus at Whittlesea.

&

Daniel "Doggy" Heal — medium height, very solid build, blonde beard and as dry and gritty as old sandpaper.

Ross, Doggy, friends and family would often spend nights around an outdoor fire playing guitar, singing songs and drinking beer.

Doggy put a horse float on his block of land after losing his house and lived in that. He should have been devoting his time to rebuilding his home and his life; instead the Kinglake Football Netball Club vice-president threw himself into helping others.

Later he was one of the organisers of the Containment Lines bushfire charity function at Crown Palladium, which raised $100,000 for local community groups. Doggy also played a key role on the club committee. Cam describes Doggy as "his rock" during the tough winter months when he was struggling psychologically.

In an era of celebrity obsession, when people seem increasingly desperate to be noticed and to get their self-satisfied smiles on TV, Doggy is refreshingly old fashioned.

One TV reporter approached him at the football club wanting to do an interview about how he was recovering from Black Saturday. Doggy respectfully declined to comment. The reporter persisted, pointing out he would be on television.

Doggy looked at him quizzically then politely asked, "Why would I want to be on television?"

In November 2009 Doggy Heal was named the Victorian Sport Volunteer of the Year.

❧

Back at the Whittlesea Relief Centre Ross decided to front the ABC and sought out presenter Libbi Gorr.

Libbi was best known by her alter ego, the comedian Elle McFeast, who after working her way through the radio ranks was eventually given her own TV show. In 2009 she was regularly on radio as an ABC relief host. Libbi was media savvy, intelligent and, most importantly in the disaster context, genuinely compassionate.

Ross spoke to her about the media circus. He complained about cameramen and journos circling like sharks waiting to feast on the slightest show of emotion. Libbi sensed Ross's need to get it off his chest, but she also knew where the story lay – with Macca, Neeve and Danny.

Any reasonable person would know how Ross was feeling, but of course they wanted to hear him actually say it. Then perhaps, for a vicarious moment or two, they would share that grief with him.

Ross went on air and told Libbi about his personal losses as well as the intrusive impact the media was having on the recovery. He told Libbi the media were upsetting a lot of people.

Libbi nailed the interview. It was such strong radio that Ross replayed it to the Kinglake footballers as they began their finals campaign in August that year. It also put the issue of media intrusiveness on the public agenda.

Two days after speaking to Libbi Gorr, and after knocking back countless other requests, Ross finally agreed to do another interview so the media would leave him alone. He decided to do a pre-record with Channel Seven's *Sunday Night* program. It was a trade-off. They wanted to know how he and Bec were coping, what they were going through.

How they felt. Ross had different priorities; he wanted the media moved away from the door at the Whittlesea Relief Centre where people came to register that they were alive, or that a loved one was still missing. As far as Ross and many others were concerned, the grief of these people was too personal to be exposed to reporters. He also urged the media to use its immense resources to take supplies up to Kinglake and other bushfire areas. "Use the helicopters to do some good," he told them.

Of course he was talking to people who had been fighting TV and radio ratings battles for years and believed they knew precisely what their audience wanted to hear and view. They weren't interested in being told by Ross Buchanan how they should use their helicopters.

Ross is unsure if Channel Seven ever put his interview to air, but one message got through. The media was moved away from the survivors the next day.

Months later Ross was still looking for walls to beat his head against.

Reporters wanted to speak to him during the local football grand final and he agreed to do an "all in" before the match started. Ross typed out an A4 sheet of notes highlighting the big recovery issues that were disturbing people in the bushfire-ravaged areas. Reporters waited patiently as Ross read through the issues. Then they asked how he felt.

Well, he felt great that Kinglake were in the grand final and it meant heaps for the local community. He was, by then, media savvy enough to know what they wanted and gave it to them in a fifteen-second grab.

CHAPTER 11

COPING

Senior Constable Caine arrived for work as normal on the Tuesday morning after the fires. He was still desperately tired and also preoccupied with what he'd be doing that day so he didn't notice the extra police cars.

His shirt and shoes were undone. At best he was scruffy. Nonchalantly, he sauntered into a police station crowded with faces he didn't recognise. It was a sea of blue with more brass than he used to carry in his plumber's van. Cam was momentarily taken aback. There was an assistant commissioner, superintendents, inspectors, dozens of constables, and before he knew it he was in the middle of them heading for his locker.

The room went silent. No one spoke, not even the senior officers. No one knew what to say so they just stared at him. Cameron tried to hide behind his locker door.

It was left to a senior constable to break the ice; he poked his head around the door and said, "There is a dress code you know!"

Cam smiled. He was with his own people, even if he didn't know a single one of them.

As he grabbed a coffee in the kitchen he could see lots of power cords running through the backyard of the station. Someone was pulling the fence down. The cavalry had arrived and the newcomers were taking charge.

Cam also learned that fellow officer Matt Wheeler and his family had survived. He was the friend that Cam and the others had unsuccessfully tried to reach when they drove down the Extons Road "fire tunnel" during that first trip back to Kinglake from Kinglake West.

A sergeant approached Cam and said they were thinking of standing him down because he lived and worked in Kinglake. The local copper resisted; Kinglakers needed him and there was no way he was going to turn his back on them. He was left alone for a while and when the sergeant returned he told Cam there was a change of plan, they were making him the community officer.

Locals had been arriving at the police station telling officers they didn't want to speak to city cops, they wanted the people they knew and trusted.

⋆

First-degree burns cause a reddening of the skin, like what happens after spending too long at the beach on a sunny day. Second-degree burns often cause the skin to blister, such as when boiling water is tipped over hands or arms. It can destroy the epidermis, the top layer of skin.

First- and second-degree burns are very painful because the endings of the nerves are impacted but still alive. Third-degree burns are of course much worse, but ironically they are not as painful. That's because the nerve endings have been entirely burned away.

With the nerves go the top two layers of skin (epidermis and dermis), sweat glands, hair follicles, some capillaries and maybe even some muscle. Because the epidermis and follicles have been destroyed new skin won't grow back. The burns victim has to undergo skin grafts, if the victim survives.

Human skin controls moisture loss and body temperature. It also provides the most important defence against germs. Once the top two layers of skin are gone the body is opened up to infection and also begins to dehydrate. Soon dehydration shuts down the kidneys and then other organs begin failing.

Patients with third-degree burns to more than 15% of their body can die. If more than 50% of the body has third-degree burns it's difficult to keep the patient alive. Jenny Clark had burns to 40% of her body. Both arms and both legs were injured as she tried desperately to get back inside the burning house.

Alfred Hospital doctors put Jenny into a coma as they pumped her full of fluids and antibiotics to help her body fight back. During the first night of surgery they struggled to keep her alive. She reacted badly to the mixture of anaesthetic and pain medication, and at one stage her heart stopped beating. After that she developed an infection and needed a twenty-four-hour intensive care nurse.

Jenny was kept in a coma for ten days. Her family came to visit and would talk to her even though she couldn't respond. There would be no reaction, at least not until Bec walked into the room.

As soon as Bec was close to her mother, Jenny's blood pressure would rise and monitors would ping differently. Bec didn't even have to say a word; she could just stand there looking at her comatose mother and the machines would come alive.

The reaction was spooky and upsetting. Bec visited less often and left it to her sister-in-law Gabe to do most of the hard yards. Gabe spent hours with Jenny chattering away about a host of issues, but there was never an acknowledgement, not a single sign, from the older woman that Gabe was ever in the ward.

Eventually Jenny briefly opened her eyes. It happened when Ross spoke. As she began to rejoin the world, she was barely coherent. She said the nurses were trying to poison her and asked Ross and Bec to remove her drip.

Ross told her he couldn't do that because the nurses had her under twenty-four-hour surveillance but he promised it was the last time their family would be told what to do by anybody. Jenny mouthed the words "I love you".

Later she insisted that federal minister and former rock star Peter Garrett had been to visit her. Jenny said the one-time Midnight Oil frontman had even sung one of his Aussie rock classics while he was in her room. The song he'd chosen for her was the hit "Beds Are Burning".

Australia can sometimes be a small world of 26 million people – Jenny Clark and Peter Garrett were to meet, coincidently, eight weeks later.

In the meantime Bec stayed in an apartment next to the Alfred so she could be close to her mother. Ross, relatives and friends visited every day to give her support. Mick was so relieved his partner for life had survived that he told her she "could have anything she wanted!"

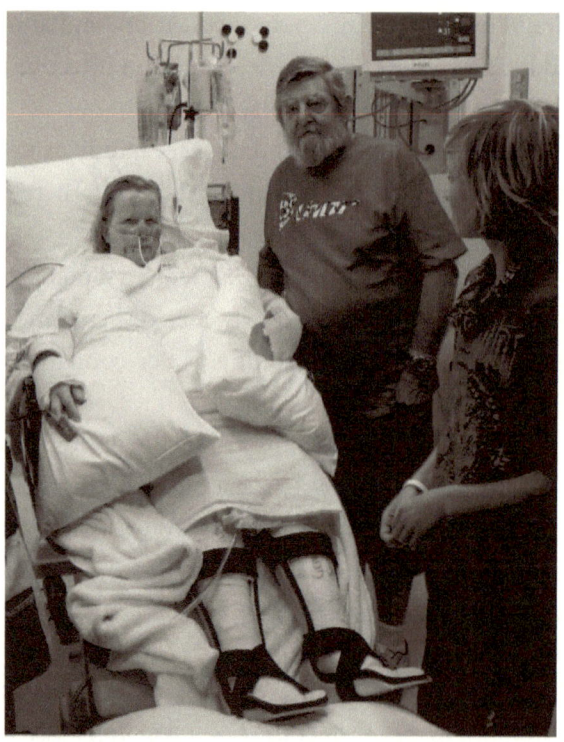

Jen, Mick and Aiden in the Alfred Hospital Burns Unit. (Pic: family collection.)

Ghosts in the Machines

The machines "coming alive" when Bec entered the hospital room of her comatose mother weren't the only technological surprise. When the battery ran out on Calum's phone and the Alfred gave Bec another one she eventually accessed her messages. There were seventy-four of them!

All those people who tried to contact her on February 7 and 8 had been flipped through to the message bank because she was either on the phone already or there was a problem with reception in the Kinglake region. At the best of times the area had poor reception and the issue was worsened by network congestion during the emergency.

Bec tried to call dozens of people, dialling hundreds of times without luck, but –
1. she got through just as the Reserve Road house was exploding into flames.
2. she was able to contact Ross when she desperately had to talk to him at Kinglake West CFA after the children died.
3. she was able to speak to Aiden inside the Kinglake CFA building.
4. on the Sunday morning when she could no longer cope by herself she got through to Dionne's phone.

Cameron Caine enjoyed a similar stroke of good luck.

His phone only worked in a few pockets up on the hill, including near the barbecue at the football clubrooms and outside his own home. He doesn't recall ever being able to make or receive a call while at the Pheasant Creek store; however, as the fire closed in on them on Black Saturday Roger Wood was able to get through with the crucial news that the road to Kinglake West was clear.

Perhaps it was where he was standing on the road that allowed him to receive the call which saved dozens of lives?

"Is that you, Aiden?"

"Yes, who's that?"

"It's Ricky Ponting."

Ross convinced Bec and Mick Clark to come out to the Whittlesea Relief Centre on the Wednesday following the fires. They were wary of the media scrum and the large numbers of people, but they also wanted to see friends.

Sporting superstars Ricky Ponting, Shane Warne and Garry Lyon were already at Whittlesea mixing with the bushfire survivors. Ross persuaded Ponting, the Australian cricket captain, to call Aiden while he was travelling to the centre.

His young son, a cricket fan, was taken aback. The phone conversation with Ponting took his mind off the tragedy that now hung ominously over the teenager's life, like the Black Saturday smoke clouds had hung over the mountain.

Mick also smiled for the first time since the fires when he was introduced to Magda Szubanski, the comedian and TV star. Besides being a very funny woman, Magda also has a warm touch about her, like the cousin you look forward to having a chat with at Christmas. She waited until the media had departed before approaching Mick and the Buchanans. It was a relaxed and a mostly cheerful few minutes amid the unrelenting gloom.

❦

In his time Shane Warne was probably the biggest star in the Australian sporting universe.

The cricket doyen became mates with Aiden Buchanan when they met at the Whittlesea Relief Centre, and they remained thick for many years. Barely a week after the fires Warne arranged for the Buchanans to fly to Sydney for a bushfire charity cricket match.

This was one of dozens of events that sprang up around Australia before February was over. Well known Aussies gave their time generously and without fee so that other Aussies would be equally generous with their hard-earned cash.

Aiden and Mick with Shane Warne at Whittlesea a few days after the fires. (Pic: family collection.)

When they reached the SCG Aiden was shocked to learn he'd be 12th man for a game that featured some of the cricketing elite. If that wasn't a big enough thrill the skipper of his team, former Australian captain Mark "Tubby" Taylor, even asked Aiden to bowl an over.

The man he was to bowl to was none less than the great Steve Waugh, tamer of the West Indian lions and England's most feared foe (other than Warnie). Aiden's feet were moving across the SCG turf but they were as light as the air.

He bowled to Waugh, who generously holed out to another former star Michael Slater. One over and one wicket for three runs. Ross said it should have been "two for" but his son was robbed of a final ball LBW.

Tubby Taylor didn't give Aiden another bowl, but it didn't matter. Aiden's life was becoming a dream, on the back of a nightmare.

But the thing about Warnie, the really good thing, is that he stayed the distance. In August 2009 when the Kinglake footballers made the grand final Shane agreed to come up and talk to them about how to win. There was only one condition: he didn't want any media involved. Not even a mention in a sports or "confidential" newspaper column.

On the night he drove to Kinglake to speak to the players it was so foggy visibility was down to about 10 metres. It was a whiteout, Warne couldn't see, and didn't know where he was. He could have been excused for turning around.

Instead he stopped the car and rang the Buchanans who eventually found the stranded sports legend and drove him to the National Park Hotel. He talked for half an hour, did a brief interview and was thanked for coming. Warne replied that he was going nowhere, not until everyone in the room had run out of questions.

So he stayed for another hour and a half. He even let some of the young women examine his hair to see if it was real. They'd seen the hair loss commercials on TV and were convinced Warnie's blonde thatch wasn't his own. He invited them to come up and give it a tug. They duly obliged and found out the hirsute coverage was the real deal, just like its owner.

When the questions were finally exhausted Shane posed for photos, and when that was finished he had a beer and a smoke outside with some of the locals before disappearing into the fog with the Buchanans.

It's not lost on the Kinglakers that while Warne contributed so much some other stars were simply too busy to venture up the mountain.

Warne continued his relationship with the Buchanans and was only ever a phone call away until his untimely death in 2022.

※

On the same Wednesday that Aiden met Ponting and Warne, Laura Caine noticed Ross on his hands and knees in the ashes at Number One Reserve Road. Life had been so hectic after the night of February 7 that she had hardly seen him since they hugged outside the Kinglake West CFA.

Now there he was back at the scene of his children's deaths, scouring the ashes of the house. What in heaven's name was he doing? Her heart quickened as she asked if he needed help. Her guess was that he probably did need help, even if he wasn't prepared to admit it.

Ross said he was on a "mission from Bec". She couldn't bear to think of any of their children's mementos lying unclaimed in the rubble heap, or worse, being scooped up and carted away to some nameless rubbish dump when the land was eventually cleared.

Laura got down on her hands and knees and helped. They searched and sifted their way through the remains of what had once been such a happy house. Tears made small dark indentations in the ash.

Eventually they found half a dozen scorched and barely recognisable medals and a few coins. Things that had once represented so much to their smiling and vibrant young owners now became sad links to times still fresh in the memory, but never to return.

Number One Reserve Road, Kinglake. (Pic: family collection.)

CHAPTER 12

NOT COPING

WHILE LAURA AND Ross were on their hands and knees looking for the children's medals, Cameron was meeting people who would play a big part in his future. Experts from the police's welfare and psych services were debriefing the Kinglake crew.

Cam and the others were warned to expect a psychological witches brew of tough times ahead. There would be flashbacks, broken sleep, memory loss, agitation, anger, tiredness and grief.

Senior Constable Caine was starting to place a tick in each box. The freight trains had been arriving each night, and the day before, the Tuesday, he had surprised himself when he broke down emotionally.

Cam had been reunited with his father, Jason, at Kinglake West CFA for the first time since the fires. When he saw his dad, freshly returned from Byron Bay, the emotions hit him like a 120-kilogram football defender. He fell into his father's arms and started crying. He told his dad he thought he was going to die and so many people had expected so much of him. Jason Caine then broke down as well. Two huge blokes stood outside the CFA building hugging and sobbing.

Then he noticed in the days ahead how he became more lethargic at work; he was easily distracted and he suffered regular memory lapses.

Much worse was to come. The senior constable was to become just a spectator at a hallucinatory show staged by his own mind.

Shortly after the fires Cameron Caine could feel someone watching him. He was home alone one afternoon eating lunch when he sensed someone staring at him. He looked over his left shoulder and found a little girl standing in the lounge room. Cameron was perplexed; he hadn't heard the dog barking or noticed any cars on the quiet dirt road.

A shiver went down his spine then spread out through his body like a river of pins and needles. At first he was startled, but he remained calm. The girl wasn't threatening in any way, but how the hell did she get inside? She wore a light-coloured dress and had fairish hair in pig tails. Silently, she stood there staring at Cameron; he sensed she was in awe of the big man in the police uniform.

He spoke to her, but there was no response. Cam felt nervous and a little disturbed, but he wasn't scared or intimidated. Slowly, he realised the youngster was an apparition. The whole episode lasted for what seemed like a few minutes before she "disappeared".

Not long afterwards he saw her again, this time while in public. Cam was standing at the football watching Kinglake when she "appeared" on the edge of the crowd staring at him.

Days later she "joined him" while he was outside at home chopping wood. She also "appeared" while he was watching a DVD in the early hours of the morning. First he seemed to sense she was in the room, and then he saw her in the murky half-light given off by the television.

Cam told no one about the "ghost", except Laura, who regarded her husband as solid and indestructible, like the Edinburgh Castle. As far as Laura was concerned, he was definitely seeing things, although precisely what the nature of those "things" were she had no idea.

Cam was certain the little girl didn't resemble Neeve Buchanan. She was about the same age with similar hair colour but Cameron had never seen Ross and Bec's little princess wearing pigtails like this girl did. Not once did she communicate with Cameron, or even appear to want to talk, she just stood there silently watching him.

If it wasn't for the police welfare people warning about flashbacks and other upsetting phenomena then he would have questioned his own mental stability. Even so, he spent hours trying to piece it all together, trying to remember the people he'd helped on Black Saturday and all the people he'd seen alive – and dead. But it was a puzzle he never solved. He never worked out who the little girl was.

Cam's police psychologist later told him it's not uncommon for people under immense stress or grief to experience transient hallucinations. Nevertheless, he was persuaded by friends to consult a spiritualist about the little girl who had been keeping him company. He travelled to the Melbourne suburb of Brunswick in November 2009 to meet with a woman who had a reputation for explaining the supernatural.

The senior constable was dismissive about the whole spiritualist process, but he had nothing to lose.

When he walked into the room the woman asked who it was he'd brought with him! Of course Cam couldn't see anyone, but the spiritualist assured him there was someone accompanying him. Cam felt light-headed. Then she told him there was a man with huge hands standing in the room alongside him, but Cameron didn't recognise the spiritualist's description of his unseen companion. Later he spoke to his mother about it and the man's description was a good fit for Cam's great-grandfather.

As for the little girl, the spiritualist told him the youngster wasn't connected to the fires and probably had something to do with where the Caines were living. Cam remained unconvinced about the whole spiritualist episode.

The welfare people were right with some of their other warnings as well. Cameron sometimes spoke to his father with such disrespect that it was as if an alien was occupying his body.

He and the family were having dinner with friends at his parents' place one night when his dad kept telling Cam about the things he needed to do at his house to get the property back in shape.

Parents invariably believe they know better than their own children what's best for them, even when their son is a senior police constable in his mid-thirties. But Cameron had other priorities in his life and the more he ignored his father the more the older man focused on his son's need to "get on with it".

When he could take it no more Cameron yelled, "Slow the fuck down!" No one spoke; they were too stunned at the outburst but at least they now had some small insight into the immense pressure that Cameron was under.

Cam was often agitated around his family, he knew it was wrong to take it out on them but he couldn't help it.

One afternoon he took a phone call from the man he helped at the football club on the night of February 7, when he'd smashed in the door to get some cold drinks. Cam was in the car with his mother and father and Laura and the boys when the call came in on his mobile phone. They were heading out for dinner.

The guy just wanted to thank him for the drinks and the reassurance he'd offered. When the conversation was over Cameron put his head against the window and looked out at the blackened hills. He was overwhelmed by emotion and began crying. Everyone else in the car went quiet. His two boys, Angus and Harry, were nonplussed until the older child reached over and, in a gesture of tactile compassion which surprised Cam, rubbed his father's knee. Cam was able to choke back the tears after that.

However, that was more the exception than the rule. The senior constable found himself tearing up regularly, sometimes in public places.

He was in the Kinglake village with Laura when someone called out his name. Cam and Laura didn't recognise the man or his wife, but they said they'd been at Pheasant Creek when the two police officers helped them to safety.

The couple gave the senior constable a big hug. Soon all three were in tears as they shared unspoken memories of just how close they'd come to death. The first weeks after the fires were full of similar chance meetings and emotional outpourings.

Life on the mountain was also exceedingly tough for the locals, who were virtual refugees in a disaster zone. There was no power and the hot weather wouldn't release its grip on the community it had helped destroy. Food deteriorated quickly. Some people had to reluctantly leave the mountain because they couldn't buy petrol locally, and on the way back up they were forced to negotiate police roadblocks. It was easier to stay home.

Many bought, or were given, generators and some enterprising local electricians hard-wired the gennies into houses, until authorities put a stop to the practice.

Ross had a slaughtered sheep and cow in his big freezer and the meat was still edible days after the fire. He shared it with friends. People shared everything they had, and leftovers were taken to the CFA building.

Because so many were reluctant to leave the mountain, coordinators at the Whittlesea Relief Centre found it difficult to help people still trying to locate friends and loved ones. Ross and others found the grapevine more helpful than the official lists.

※

Cam began seeing his doctor the week after the fires. He regaled Dr Greg with a verbal cavalcade of horror.

At one stage Dr Greg's eyes welled up and Cam thought he was going to start crying, but the medico held his nerve and the consultations continued over a number of weeks. However, Cameron was getting worse, not better. The apparitions hadn't gone away, nor had the sleepless and seemingly endless nights. He would stay up until four in the morning watching movies and trying to hold the demons at bay. If sleep eventually claimed him, then the horrific nightmares would begin.

Olfactory senses shut down during sleep, that's why people often don't smell fires. But each time Cam went to sleep he believed he could smell the smoke. It was that real. Even in his waking moments when he was alone in the police car he would visualise the flames, relive the moments, and the terror would return.

Perhaps most disturbing of all his sex drive had gone crazy, it was insatiable. It was bizarre. Senior Constable Caine needed more help.

❧

Jenny wanted to hear some music, and she wanted Ross to play it. Eleven days after her life-saving surgery she was placed in a mechanical monstrosity, a sort of half bed-half wheelchair contraption and taken down to the Alfred Hospital cafeteria where her family was waiting.

Jenny and family lasted only a few bars of the melancholic Pink Floyd song "Wish You Were Here" before bursting into tears. It had been Danny Clark's favourite song.

Then Ross played "Beautiful Creation", a song he'd written with Neeve. With determination, he persevered and belted out a few more tunes before he and Jenny were emotionally drained. She was then wheeled back to the Intensive Care Unit.

Slowly Jenny was making progress. Bec spent so much time with her mother that she became familiar with the dressing and bandaging of the wounds. Sometimes Jenny would shower and then the pair of them would have to sit around and wait for a nurse to do the dressings, so soon enough Bec was doing the bandaging.

Bec also fed her mother because Jenny couldn't lift her arms. Over the weeks Jenny was able to do a little bit more each day and eventually she could put a spoon to her mouth. After six weeks the doctors wanted to send her to rehab in Caulfield, on the south-east side of Melbourne. But Jenny wanted out. There's no one less patient than a hospital patient who wants to go home!

Because Jenny was eventually going to stay at the Buchanans' house, where there are three stairs, the specialists told her she could leave if she could prove to them that she could climb a staircase.

Single-mindedly, and in great pain, she got stuck into it. At first it was just a centimetre at a time but slowly Jenny's body adjusted until finally she conquered the staircase and proclaimed she was ready to leave. However, the evening before she was due to go home nurses told Jenny she would have to stay longer. She was livid, but what they couldn't disclose was that her football hero, Nathan Buckley, was making a surprise visit.

The following day Bec, Ross and other family members came to see her wearing Collingwood colours. Still she didn't guess what was happening, Jenny just assumed they were proud Magpie supporters.

Then Buckley, the former Collingwood skipper, turned up and for a moment Jenny beamed like there was no yesterday. It was the perfect going home present.

In 2010 Collingwood made the AFL Grand Final and Mick and Jenny postponed a trip overseas so they could see their beloved Magpies in action. The game finished in a frustrating draw and had to be replayed the following week. Mick and Jenny couldn't delay their trip any longer so they made arrangements to view Grand Final #2 while they were overseas. But Mick became confused about the time difference and they ended up missing the game entirely. Collingwood won its first flag in twenty years. Buckley, by then retired, was an assistant coach.

There were no tall poppies in Australia in the weeks after the fires.

Australia's sporting, artistic and political elite were only too happy to reach out and provide whatever momentary relief their celebrity status offered the bushfire victims.

Shane Warne was a dynamo. He rang Aiden and said he was heading back up the mountain but this time he wanted to go to Flowerdale and he was bringing a friend.

The one-time "Sheik of Tweak", as Warnie was dubbed, turned up at Flowerdale Primary School with Coldplay's Chris Martin. The Buchanans then took the singer and the cricketer to Flowerdale's temporary village and the local pub, which had miraculously survived the fires.

Martin was rendered almost speechless by the endless scenes of utter desolation during the drive along the Whittlesea-Yea Road through the Flowerdale valley. He quietly took it all in. When it was finished Ross gave him a copy of his CD *Cobbers*. Martin responded by reaching inside their car and exchanging *Cobbers* for Pink Floyd's *Dark Side of the Moon*.

CHAPTER 13

NEW GOALS

CAMERON CAINE TURNED to the football field for some mental relief. He remained president of the Kinglake Football Netball Club and played at full forward in the Reserves team. Fans watching Cameron said he was playing like a man possessed. They didn't know how close they were to the truth.

His 100 minutes on the footy field were his day release from the mental prison he found himself in with so many of his waking thoughts consumed by the fire and its aftermath. On the field he would crash packs and manhandle opponents with inspired violence. There were no fists or elbows, just an unrelenting attack on the ball, or the man with the ball. Football became his refuge, and he became increasingly grateful that the people of Kinglake hadn't sent their club into recess for the season.

About a week after the fires people had begun asking the Kinglake Football Netball Club president if the teams would be playing in 2009.

The vice-president, Doggy Heal, was living in a horse float after losing his house. Dionne Smith, who was also on the club committee, had lost her house. Secretary Lynn Normington still had her home, but like so many others was lucky to have survived. She was holding her daughter's party on the afternoon of February 7 when one of the mums arrived and said everyone needed to get out, the fire was at Kinglake!

Impossible, thought Lynn, who lives about a kilometre north of the village, just off Glenburn Road and not far from where Cam and Roger found the abandoned CFA truck. Soon enough the advancing flames put an end to the party and Lynn quickly packed kids and animals into her car and made her getaway. She headed north for Glenburn. Embers were bouncing off the vehicle and she was concerned the fire was going to overtake them. When she reached Glenburn there were cars lined up along the roadside, their occupants relieved to have found safety.

She wasn't convinced. There was more smoke away to her right from the huge Murrindindi fire. Lynn, kids and animals kept going all the way to Yea where she was certain the fire couldn't touch them.

Everyone on the Kinglake committee had been affected in some way by the tragedy, and everyone knew of someone who'd perished. Cam consulted the club treasurer, Laura. Together, with one or two others, they had kept the club going as it limped through its final year in the tough Northern Football League. Since transferring to the Yarra Valley Mountain District League in 2008, where they played against other country towns, they had enjoyed some success.

Laura wanted the club to continue for the season. Her belief was that the community would need somewhere to go to get away from their burnt homes, properties and problems for a few hours every Saturday. Laura also needed to keep her mind occupied with matters other than the scars that the fire had left on her community. Cameron was not so convinced.

The Caines knew it wasn't really their decision to make and arranged to hold a town meeting on February 19 so the players and the community could decide the fate of the Kinglake Football Netball Club.

Deep down they weren't even sure people could be bothered turning up and voting but, perhaps in a harbinger of the season that was to unfold, nearly 200 people arrived at the ground.

Someone who looked very much like former football star Jimmy Stynes moved among the crowd. Young people stared at him. It *was* Jimmy Stynes!

The giant Irishman, former Brownlow Medallist and Melbourne Football Club president, turned up with Demon chief executive Cameron Schwab and some of the players to support the people of Kinglake. They even brought up a couple of ute loads of gear. Kids were incredulous as the professional Melbourne players handed out footballs and training tops. Laker players, families and fans sensed that there were people off the mountain who were interested in their wellbeing and perhaps would even support them.

Jimmy Stynes addressed the crowd in his lyrical Irish brogue and told them the footy world was behind them. People cheered.

Then it was Cameron's turn. "All those who feel that to play on in 2009 would be just too much for people to cope with please raise your hands." Silence. Not a single hand went up. Nervously, Cameron asked for a show of hands from all those who "feel the club should go ahead and play on this season".

A forest of arms shot into the air. It was unanimous. The young men and women of Kinglake would play football and netball!

In the background army trucks were parked on the oval, the ground surface was as hard as concrete, the ticket box and storage shed were destroyed, the water tanks were leaking, floodlights drooped on burnt wires from their wooden poles and, nearly a fortnight after the fires, some logs and stumps still smouldered. Voting was the easy part.

Cam and younger son Harry at the Kinglake community meeting. (Pic: News Corp.)

From that moment on Jimmy Stynes was a friend of Kinglake. His success on and off the football field and his deep reserves of mental strength inspired trust. The Irishman played a record 244 consecutive games of footy for the Demons, refusing to succumb to injuries that would normally ground an AFL high-flyer.

Jimmy was blessed with a common touch and was thought of as a people's champion. An uncle had been a national hero in the IRA, something Jimmy had written about, and after retiring from footy he devoted himself to charity work with his youth foundation Reach.

Jimmy and the other Demons had travelled through the police roadblocks and up the mountain without being called on for a favour. It wasn't a marketing project or exercise in media manipulation; it was simply a case of good people reaching out. So it came as a cruel blow later in the season when news broke that Jimmy was suffering from cancer and faced the battle of his life to survive.

Like thousands of other people, Kinglakers were in a state of shock and the news cast an air of despondency over a club that had already suffered more than its share of adversity. Players signed a card and Laura had a Kinglake jumper framed and sent to Jimmy.

The message from many who had survived the fight of their lives was that they were with the Big Fella heart and soul. Jimmy Stynes died in 2012.

It was sometime in the weeks after the fire that Cameron Caine's role as a president of the Kinglake Football Netball Club (KFNC) began to chew up almost as much time as his work in the blue uniform.

KFNC is the largest organisation on the Kinglake ridge, bigger even than any of the primary schools. It was set to play a major role in the recovery, and consequently Cam was unknowingly assuming the role of a community leader. The media chased him for comment and people he'd never met began phoning up with offers of help. Cameron didn't know it yet but his life was heading in a new direction.

Donors wanted to give money to the club because they believed its members would be well placed to know who the neediest people were in the Kinglake community. Some just wanted to give money to the "footy club".

Cam, Laura and Doggy Heal sat down one afternoon and talked about what they would do with the dollars. Their decision would later leave some football executives incredulous: they would give it all away.

Doggy approached a mate from an entertainment company, Matthew Banks, to help organise a charity night. They called it Containment Lines, as in "fire containment lines". Former footy star Billy Brownless, TV and radio host Angela Pippos, comedian Dave O'Neill, the irascible AFL headliner Brendan Fevola and other media and sporting heavyweights agreed to support it. In just a few weeks they gathered sporting memorabilia to auction off, sold tables and conjured up a major entertainment extravaganza that normally would have taken months to organise.

They raised $100,000 for the community.

Fevola, a football star with a wild-man reputation, was fantastic. He spent time with the Kinglake crew after the night had officially finished and indulged them in an impromptu bout of homespun "wrestlemania".

Nine months earlier the controversial former Carlton star had attended a Laker function on a Sunday afternoon and spent hours kicking a football around with the local kids. Although he consumed only a few beers on the day, he was stung by media reports that he was on the grog again. Someone had put him in.

The Lakers had nothing but good things to say about Fevola and Cam couldn't help thinking that the footy superstar was just a suburban boy trying to stay afloat in a very public fishbowl.

The efforts of Fevola and the others helped push the club's Bushfire Appeal fund up towards $150,000, and they began giving the money away to emergency services and local schools – groups they knew needed immediate support.

Thousands of dollars also went to community dining. Locals, with council support, had set up dining areas at Kinglake and Kinglake West where people could buy a meal for just a few dollars. These eateries were crowded out at night. Hundreds of people would come in from their caravans or tents or the cramped homes they were sharing with others and spend time eating and talking with friends.

It was a quasi-refugee situation, and it was only an hour's drive from Melbourne, where people were buying lattes and flat screen TVs and takeaway meals as per normal. Inevitably, the rest of the world was moving on.

❧

To its long-lasting credit the AFL, with help from the Victorian Country Football League and the local competition, bankrolled an administrator to take some of the pressure off Cam and the committee so they could focus on their bushfire recovery. The idea of sending in some help came from the general manager of the local Yarra Valley Mountain District League, Stephen Walter, who knew that a healthy football and netball club was a hallmark of a healthy community.

Together the administrator and the committee turned their focus to round one, a match against Emerald, which was barely a month away. They decided to make it a day for the whole community, a chance for friends and relatives to catch up and forget their problems for a couple of hours.

Although there had been lots of functions off the mountain, to raise money or to remember those who'd lost their lives, many locals had missed out. It was too far for them to travel and the roadblocks were intrusive. But this match on April 4 would be organised by the locals, for the locals. There would be a minute's silence before the game, they would invite emergency services to parade on the oval and they would get someone special to sing the national anthem.

Committee members threw up some big names. What about pop divas Kylie Minogue or Natalie Imbruglia? Midnight Oil fan Cameron Caine suggested Peter Garrett, the former rock star turned politician. But Garrett was a federal minister, an earnest and responsible member of the Australian Government who'd long since moved on from his earlier years of manically inspired stage gyrations. Nevertheless, they decided to try Garrett. Within a week he'd said yes!

The AFL had also invited Kinglake people to attend a NAB Cup match between Essendon and the Bulldogs at Docklands Stadium. Families were bussed into the city and put up by the AFL at local hotels.

On the way to the ground the kids rolled on green grass at one of the city parks. They laughed and giggled at how soft and lush the vegetation was.

Inside the huge stadium Kinglakers were asked out onto the playing arena before the game and stood alongside AFL team captains. Aiden Buchanan tossed the coin while his father stood nearby. Ross looked a lonely and forlorn figure. There was no joy in the moment, just a sense of grief and unbearable loss.

A hush came over the stadium, thousands of fans watching in respectful silence, the only sound coming from the dull hum of the city in the background. If Cameron was becoming a community spokesman, Ross was quickly becoming a figurehead for Black Saturday grief.

Later Cam, Doggy, Ross and some of the others went back to their motel units in the inner suburbs and had a few drinks. Cam sat outside on a fire hydrant taking in the night when suddenly there was a power failure. Only car lights lit up the darkness. Cam began sweating and started to panic. He quickly retreated to the security of his room.

Much later Ross headed to his room; an early edition of the *Herald Sun* newspaper was waiting at his door. He was on the front page with Laura and another Kinglake Football Netball Club friend, Janine McAllister. Ross didn't want to become public property, it wasn't a role he sought for himself but when he didn't say "no" often enough he found himself on a media journey not of his choosing.

It would lead all the way to a *60 Minutes* TV appearance and a "tyre lever" threat.

◆

Media file – listing under – "Kinglake victims – Ross and Rebecca Buchanan, fill-in address/ phone numbers/background/other contacts."

The Buchanans were always going to attract media attention because of the heart shattering nature of their losses. But a number of factors also served to put them firmly in the public spotlight. Kinglake is much closer to Melbourne than the other major fire disaster zone, Marysville, and so was easier for the media to reach. Marysville was cut off for much longer, and with the village virtually wiped out it was harder to trace victims. The Kinglake ridge also had a bigger population than the other major fire-impacted areas.

Ross, with his desire to put the record straight, also quickly became a "victim" the journalists were familiar with. In contrast to her husband, Bec was out of the public eye because she was spending every day with her mother at the Alfred. When eventually she began doing some media the reporters were already well aware of who she was. One newspaper reporter even rang her up later in the year for a comment about the Greg Norman–Chris Evert marriage break-up because Bec had briefly met the sporting legends!

But it was Ross who made most of the running as he sought to engage the media on his own terms. For example, Channel Nine staff worked frantically to put together a bushfire appeal within a week of the disaster. On the appeal night Bec, Ross, Aiden and Calum were meeting country music star Adam Brand at Whittlesea.

Adam gave Calum a Maton guitar and then they all wandered over to the Disaster Relief Centre to check out the Nine show. Ross picked up on the positive energy of the evening and told a Nine producer he wanted to get involved – "Let me get up on stage and sing to my community."

He kept harassing the guy until the producer relented and after a brief audition was put in front of the cameras on national TV to sing one of his own songs, "Salty Tears". However, Ross ignored his cue to start singing and instead asked the crowd to show their red wrist bands. People living in the fire zones had to wear the wrist bands to get through the roadblocks. As Ross suspected, only a few hands went into the air. The vast majority of the crowd at the Nine show were not bushfire survivors. Those people were either stranded on the mountain without transport or were too busy to attend because they were picking up the pieces of their lives. Ross decided he would sing for them on television.

He rode the euphoria of the occasion until near the end of the song when the emotion of the night began to cave in on him. He thought he was on top of it, but he was so far away he couldn't even see the summit.

Ross left the stage and collapsed into the arms of the nearest person, who happened to be a woman from the police band. Then he bawled his eyes out. Producers prevented the song going live to air, but footage turned up the following night in the news.

Ross went over to Bec and was soon surrounded by fifteen of Macca's mates. Once he'd composed himself he began talking to the group and gave them a pep talk about pulling through together. Ross felt like he was coaching an underage footy team again and he told the boys the media would probably be interested in what they did next and they should decide how they would mark the disaster.

The kids came up with the idea that they'd all wear bandanas like Macca used to. They ordered a thousand and sold them to raise money for a plaque at a Yea skate park to be built in honour of Macca.

Ross was gaining hands-on awareness of how the media works, or more importantly, how to make it work for him. Soon hundreds of students at Yea and Whittlesea Colleges were wearing bandanas, and even some of the staff at Yea put on the head gear.

CHAPTER 14

RISING FROM THE ASHES?

JENNY CLARK CAME home on April 2, nearly two months after the fires. She and Mick stayed in the main bedroom at the Buchanan home in National Park Road. Ross and Bec slept in Macca's room.

Ross worked through a veil of tears to clean out the room. He had to focus hard to stay rational. Wild emotions were rattling his cage. Each item in the bedroom had meant something important to his son and to move any one of them was somehow breaking a bond with the past. But the focus had to be on the present.

Bec volunteered to help the Christian group Global Care, which had set up an office in Kinglake. Dozens of Global Care volunteers from around Australia flew in to assist the disaster victims. Bec was surprised to learn that Global Care applied the same classification to the Kinglake ridge in its time of emergency as it did to a developing country. This was because there was no running water. Without electricity household pumps couldn't be powered, and even if they did have generators most of the water tanks were polluted with ash and soot.

Global Care staff were well received by the locals because they didn't ask questions, nor did they demand the completion of copious amounts of paperwork, which infuriated people already on short fuses. The Christian aid workers simply "got stuck in" and Bec lent her time to them whenever she could.

As the weeks wore on Bec noticed that people were becoming less patient with aid workers, and with each other. One woman complained that her washing machine had broken down, and although her house had survived the fires, she asked Bec to supply a new one.

Bec said Global Care couldn't do that. Impatiently, the woman, who didn't recognise her, shot back "You have no idea what I'm going through!" Bec could have spent the whole afternoon telling her what *she* was going through, but she didn't bother.

She was planning to bury two children and a brother. She was helping her badly burned mother and surviving children. She was coping with a husband who was sometimes an emotional mess and was drinking beer every day.

In fact, Ross was hitting the grog like a thirty-five-year-old footballer on his last end-of-season trip with the boys. Bec didn't drink or smoke and her husband's behaviour was just one more irritant in a life overflowing with torments. Months later, at the end of November, it came to a head when Ross was drunk five nights in a row. On one occasion he forgot to pick up Aiden and didn't know where his son was.

Bec told him it was bullshit and it had to finish. Ross knew she was right.

But there were small signs of progress a month after the fires. Wally had cleared up the backyard, Aiden said he was ready to return to school and he had also been invited to train alongside the Collingwood footballers.

While Aiden was kicking the football, the Collingwood Club president and media industry luminary Eddie McGuire took Mick out for lunch. In the rarefied world of Aussie sporting culture and its millions of obsessive adherents, that's about as good as it gets.

There was more traffic along National Park Road.

In fact, there was too much traffic. Tourists were coming up from town to gaze in awe at the aftermath of the conflagration and take photos of a disaster zone so they could show friends and family how horrible it was. They were just thankful it was somebody else's problem.

One car struck the Buchanans' cat. The cat used up its second life at a cost of $700 in vet's bills.

Locals felt like they were part of the Kinglake scenery, part of the backdrop for a tourist photo op.

※

Within a kilometre of the Buchanans' house stands a building that, on the hottest days, looks like a shimmering golden mirage. It's a three storey Buddhist temple sitting incongruously in farmland behind the National Park Road houses. Ross, Neeve and their dog Jazz would often walk there for some exercise and simply to marvel close-up at a remarkable piece of architecture.

Although fires swept in from two directions on Black Saturday, the magnificent building survived unscathed. As March turned to April the Buddhists held a simple but moving ceremony in memory of the victims.

Police chief Christine Nixon was among those who attended and afterwards Ross asked her to come home and meet his mother-in-law. Jenny Clark had worked at the Police Forensic Unit in Macleod and her service plaque, signed by Nixon, had been lost in the fires.

Nixon, who was retiring from the police force, had agreed to chair the Victorian Bushfire Relief and Reconstruction Authority (VBRRA), and was deeply touched by all that Jenny had been through.

The Buchanans and the top cop were to meet many times in the months ahead, and they were there with Ms Nixon when her life threatened to fall apart as the media came after her in 2010.

Ross was also concerned that the local government body, Murrindindi Shire, was not doing all it could to help Nixon and the VBRRA staff.

He placed the shire on the same blacklist as the media. Ross alleged the shire blocked the distribution of "free stuff" so local businesses wouldn't suffer and also discouraged survivors from the Canberra bushfires from offering assistance.

He was difficult to deal with, and sometimes aggressive, in the weeks and months after the fires. In fact, it's likely Ross was on some blacklists himself. Certainly if Prime Minister Kevin Rudd's people were watching closely when the two men met for the first time, Ross would have been placed in the handle-with-care basket.

Before Jenny came home Ross went to the Kinglake West aid centre one day in late February to get some drinking water. The cat was thirsty! He was holding two beers and a cigarette when the PM's motorcade pulled in. The pair was introduced and while Mr Rudd focused on expressing his sorrow for the sufferings of the Buchanan family, Ross was after some concessions. He demanded a regular bus service for people along the Kinglake ridge and, somewhat bizarrely given the circumstances of the meeting, free sport for kids in a bid to counter childhood obesity.

The prime minister politely moved on. He wasn't about to debate a guy armed with two beers, a cigarette and a feisty attitude who was mourning the loss of two children.

(Bus services along the Kinglake ridge improved dramatically following that impromptu meeting, but there was no word on the abolition of fees for kids' sport.)

In March and April, Ross and Wally also spent their days setting up a free firewood project for the locals. They knew the icy Kinglake winter would be upon most people before they were ready. Crews working on the nearby huge North-South pipeline project donated man hours and machinery to construct a timber yard, and the Whittlesea Lions Club chipped in loads of red gum. Most took only as much wood as they could use, but others were hauling away so much Ross suspected they may have been going into business for themselves.

Later in the year locals were upset by the mass clearing of burnt trees from along the roadsides and burnt properties. A member of the big Exton family allowed the trees to be stacked in his paddocks. There was so much timber the trees formed windrows hundreds of metres long. To the dismay of Ross and Wally workers then began wood-chipping the trees. Wally fronted the authorities and demanded local people be allowed to use the logs for firewood. But perhaps most importantly of all, Ross was staying busy and his focus was on the present. He, and Cam, became heavily involved in preparations for the opening of the football and netball season.

※

Planning for the "Rising from the Ashes" round one football and netball clash was gaining momentum. Peter Garrett, fellow federal MP Bill Shorten, Victorian Premier John Brumby and Christine Nixon had accepted invitations along with musicians Adam Brand, Bob Evans and others.

The committee had no way of knowing how many thousands would turn up at the game or the after-match rock concert, which club members Brooke Coleman and Tegan Smith had organised. No one had any experience with an event of these proportions.

Compounding the growing list of problems, there was no rain and the ground was rock hard so there was a chance the footy would have to be called off. Also the coroner wasn't convinced that all the missing people had been accounted for and ordered the roadblocks to stay in place. Consequently, Kinglake remained in lockdown mode except for locals and visitors with special wristband passes.

Murrindindi Shire also had concerns about the dozens of burned trees at the oval, which it regarded as a safety hazard. So, while the media was promoting Kinglake's big coming-out- day Cam and the committee had to consider postponing the match or even calling it off. People were getting nervous.

But the problems they were facing were insignificant compared to the life changing events they'd been through.

Cameron got to work organising some mates to knock over the dead trees at the oval and a crew from Shepparton donated their time to repair the sprinkler system water pump and switchboard, which had been destroyed on February 7.

Ross then threw himself into watering the ground and although he could only get one third of the sprinklers working, he put so much water on the moisture-starved surface that he partly flooded it.

Unfortunately, everywhere he looked on the Kinglake ridge he could see traces of his children. Teachers from Kinglake Middle School who had known Neeve came to chat while he was working on the water pump. In the weeks and months ahead those teachers, and the principal Janette Cook, were always there for the Buchanans. Memorial artwork was completed for Neeve and when quilts were donated to the school one was put aside for the deceased youngster.

As he watered the ground ahead of the big game Ross stood and watched the school children playing on the oval. The kids laughed and screamed with barely a care in the world as they ran through his sprinklers. Life is a bit like water, always moving on.

Two nights before the big match the club, with the generous support of a catering company, put on a free dinner for all the emergency service workers who'd helped on Black Saturday. Hundreds of people were at the ground and the place was humming. TV crews filmed the night and there was a distinct feeling the community was moving forward with its recovery.

Ross spent some time with Channel Seven reporter Nick McCallum. Nick's first question was "How do you feel?" Ross knew the question was coming and knew how he was going to answer. He took Nick down to Pine Ridge Road and showed him where people had died. He pointed out that half the town and half his family were gone. Ross's eyes never left Nick's face. He watched the veteran reporter closely and for just a couple of seconds detected that the other man "got it".

Ross then told Nick, "OK. That's how I feel, every moment of every day." For the first time Ross was happy with the way he was portrayed on TV.

The following day, round one eve, more water went onto the ground. Local water contractor, Charles Exton, who'd help save people in his "High Mountain" sheds on the night of the fires, sent his big tankers up and they tipped another 60,000 litres onto the oval.

Then of course it rained heavily. The ground surrounds turned to mud. But that didn't stop locals turning up en masse the following day. Two and a half thousand people were at the match, the biggest crowd to ever attend a local game. There were hugs and smiles and tears.

Bill Shorten, the federal parliamentary secretary for the bushfires and former union boss, wandered out by himself from behind the pavilion where he'd parked and said "G'day" to anybody who wanted to have a chat.

Ross Buchanan and Bill Shorten have some history. The previous year Ross had sung at a Labor Party fund raiser that the MP attended. They sat at the same table and, not realising it was a BYO function, Ross had enthusiastically helped himself to Bill's beer without asking.

Later in 2009 Shorten was at another Kinglake football match when the governor general, Quentin Bryce, was invited into the change rooms to speak to the players who were in various stages of undress. Ross remarked quietly to Shorten that Ms Bryce would probably be a bit frisky that night.

Ross didn't realise Bill Shorten is married to the governor general's daughter, and the two men haven't spoken since that day. The apparent chill between them may have been exacerbated by Ross's tendency to fire off vitriolic emails slamming Shorten, and others, over bushfire recovery issues, although Shorten only ever had the community's best interests at heart.

Peter Garrett, living testimony that you can't take the rock star out of the politician, particularly when you're a giant of a man with a shaved head, immediately attracted a crowd when he arrived at the Kinglake ground. Fans flowed around him like an incoming tide.

People also gathered around Victorian Premier Brumby, but they seemed more discerning in their conversations, with some intent on detailing the perceived failings of the state government and their concerns about bushfire recovery. As usual the premier took it in his stride, prompting some to remark that his handlers must paint his smile on at the start of the day.

Not far away Christine Nixon had a relaxed chat with the locals. Out of her police uniform and in her new bushfire supremo role, she smiled and looked happy to have finally let her personality out to play.

The dignitaries worked behind the stalls and flipped hamburgers. Certainly it was great folksy TV for the six o'clock news, but the big wigs were very much at home with the people who'd lost everything. Like millions of other Australians they just wanted to help in the time of need.

Ross helps Peter Garrett sing the national anthem at Rising from the Ashes. (Pic: Nic Gibson, Fairfax.)

Out on the ground Cam Caine and the Kinglake Reserves skipper Ben Collins were desperately trying to give the town the fairytale win it craved over Emerald in the curtain raiser to the main game. The Lakers were playing in commemorative black and grey bushfire jumpers with the words "7th February 2009" emblazoned on the front. They were chasing a win they felt they owed the community; losing the game given all that they'd been through together was simply unthinkable.

They lost.

Caine and Collins collapsed in each other's arms and teared up. The cameras clicked merrily away. Cameron then had only a few minutes to compose himself before he was required up on stage with the guests.

A torrent of emotion was coursing through his body, the loss to Emerald, the thought of sharing the moment with Ross, the pressure of making an unprepared speech in front of some heavy hitters; it was all coming together at the wrong time.

He had his head in his hands a number of times. Thousands of eyes were on him and the unforgiving TV cameras were lapping it up. Thankfully the emergency service people were welcomed onto the ground along with the players and he had some extra minutes to calm himself.

The CFA, the ambos, the SES and others came together to soak up the accolades they had earned for their battle against the overwhelming forces of nature less than two months earlier. They were so joyous, so happy to be among friends and family in front of a small audience of applauding dignitaries.

For a moment the fires and the tragedy seemed a long way off. Cameron knew then that no matter what the season held for Kinglake on the playing fields they had already had the biggest win of all.

A smile came to his face. Smiles came to thousands of faces. But it was one thing for Cameron to release his frustrations on the football field and then speak publicly for ten minutes, it was significantly more demanding for Ross to have to jolly-up and sing for half an hour. There had even been some debate as to whether he should be asked at all to perform in front of thousands of people. But it was his club and they were his friends, family and neighbours, and seeing and hearing Ross perform on stage became a poignant moment as the community looked to come to terms with the events of February 7.

If they could look at him on stage they could look him in the eye in the street as well and perhaps reach a mutual and implicit understanding that somehow life goes on.

As the crowd relaxed and smiled, so did Ross; he had put plenty of thought into the most appropriate way to handle the situation. Somewhere in his psychological make-up there's an irreverent gene, a naughty gene that compels him to do things such as mock a federal minister while they were on stage together preparing to sing the Australian national anthem.

To the amusement of thousands he gave his stilted impression of Garrett singing the national anthem circa 1985. People laughed and cheered. The ice was broken at the most solemn community moment since the disaster.

Garrett had only agreed to sing the anthem if the public helped out. It was a pre-condition that people found irresistible and they joined in with gusto singing a theme song for the nation. A theme song for those who believe, despite our occasional differences, we're all in this together.

Cameron then somehow strung together enough sensible sentences to get the job done and Shorten, Garrett and Brumby all made speeches before it was back to Ross who was in his comfort zone alongside his band Pay Dirt.

His irreverent gene gained the upper hand again and to the cheers of the locals he demanded the politicians "give us back our petrol station". Since the fires destroyed the servo locals had been travelling off the mountain to Whittlesea or Yarra Glen to fill up. It was a round trip of at least fifty kilometres.

Ross then belted out his Kinglake song and each time he reached the chorus, thousands, including the politicians, joined in with the refrain "Kinglake is where I wannabe".

Even for the tone deaf among the audience it was one of those unforgettable occasions when it was more awkward not to contribute than to have a stab at singing the chorus. Cam and Ross embraced on the stage in a moment that symbolised the day.

The searing events of February 7 welded Cam and Ross into a steely relationship of mutual dependence, although as the months wore on it was more often Ross calling his mate for advice or a sympathetic ear. They would also seek to work together as their lives regained more balance.

As far as their township was concerned Kinglake wasn't exactly Rising from the Ashes, but it was starting to move forward.

Jenny Clark also had a smile on her face that day. She met Garrett and gave him a firsthand account of the "Beds Are Burning" story, telling him how he'd pranced into her room at the Alfred Hospital and sung the song that had pricked the conscience of a nation two decades earlier. And now here he was in the flesh, standing in front of her at Kinglake. Life sure deals up some unlikely hands sometimes.

A couple of days earlier Jenny and Mick had slipped quietly up to the clubrooms for a meal. People were happy and relieved to see them back in the community but were keen to get on with things. There would be an appropriate time to allow their hearts to weep tears in the weeks ahead. The coroner had yet to release the bodies of the two children and Dan.

Cam and Ross embrace on stage at Rising from the Ashes. (Pic: Nic Gibson, Fairfax.)

CHAPTER 15

THE HARDEST THING

KINGLAKE'S LOCAL POLICE made a pact among themselves to attend every funeral they could possibly get to. It was like being caught in a chamber of tragedy. It wore them down. One day a funeral for someone they all knew, the next for a family of four including two young children. Two Auskick kids and both their parents gone forever. It didn't seem possible.

Instead of being filled with talk about footy, or changes at work or even some juicy gossip, their days were replete with words of bereavement.

Cam and Roger met with police welfare every Tuesday and back-tracked over the events of February 7 and 8. But Cam felt like he was operating on automatic pilot. Only family and football were giving his life some direction. At times he would be chopping wood in the backyard at home and would find himself vacantly staring off into the distance. The footy club had purchased some green and gold wrist bands with the words "Kinglake – we won't be beaten". To bring himself back to reality Cam would stretch the wrist band as tight as he could and release it so it snapped back against his forearm stinging him.

Eventually he told the welfare people he couldn't continue in the job, he was going to take a break after the funerals of the Buchanan children.

Senior Constable Caine, former plumber and roughneck full forward also took the plunge into unknown territory: he asked for psychological help. The little girl he kept seeing, his impatience with his children, the lack of sleep and the vivid dreams… it was all overwhelming him.

There was also that insatiable sexual appetite. He served it up to Laura at every opportunity with a lukewarm heart and no lashings of romance.

Cam found an empathetic ear when he met the psych, Nancy, and the more he confided in her the more her answers and explanations made good sense. However, he was decidedly uncomfortable discussing his sex life with anyone, it was a betrayal of the trust that he and Laura shared.

Eventually, after a few meetings he nervously revealed how he was driving Laura to distraction. Nancy didn't flinch and there was certainly no "nudge, nudge" smile. She was warm but also clinical and explained to Cameron that sexual urges were a natural reaction after so much devastation and death. Nancy told him there's a "need to feel alive and a need for human companionship and intimacy. It can also be a way of communicating a range of emotions which cannot otherwise be expressed or verbalised."

She added that birth is the opposite of death and it's common for the birth rate to jump after disasters. Three Kinglake club members had babies in November 2009, nine months after the disaster, and the feeling of renewal and moving forward was palpable.

Cam walked out of every meeting with Nancy marvelling at her ability to reduce complex issues into common sense answers. About the same time he also agreed to start taking anti-depressants; he was willing to concede that the "scotch and Coke" self-medication wasn't working.

He was making progress.

Bec and Ross also seemed to be taking very small steps forward. They came around with Wally one afternoon to ask Cameron some searching questions about the deaths of Macca and Neeve.

Bec revealed that her birthday was the same day as Neeve's, November 27, a date she had treasured each year and looked forward to as it drew closer on the calendar. But now, and forever more, it would be a date to dread, a day weighed down with heavy memories that would become a little bit lighter as the years rolled by.

Ross looked at the ground as his wife spoke. This was the day that Bec summoned up the courage to ask Cameron to tell as much as he knew about the deaths. Although he obliged her Cam did withhold one key fact. He didn't reveal to the Buchanans until months later that it was actually him who found the bodies.

❦

When November 27, 2009, eventually arrived Bec decided not to sit around mourning the loss of her daughter. No way was she going to turn the house into a candle-lit shrine with the focus on photos of the pretty little blonde girl. No way. They were going to have a birthday celebration. Bec invited more than 100 people to their National Park Road home.

Landscapers had been hard at work putting in a new lawn and concrete area at the back of the house. They had also built a wooden amphitheatre on the edge of the forest where Ross and Wally and the others could play their instruments while they sat around a warming fire.

The night was bursting with energy, lots of friends chatting and getting louder as alcohol turned up the volume. It was all positive stuff, even when the birthday cake was cut. Dionne's daughter Kelsey and two of Neeve's little cousins, Genna and Tarnee, did the honours.

But they may as well have cut into the hearts of the throng that gathered around to watch and sing happy birthday. Inevitably, as soon as the focus moved to Neeve, it became a desperately sad occasion.

Importantly though, the Kinglake people were there for each other, as well as for Ross and Bec. Soon enough they returned to drinking and socialising and enjoying themselves. Then they meandered off home when they thought things were about as right as they could be under the circumstances.

In the days after November 27 there was a role reversal in the Buchanan household. Previously Bec had been stoic and even tempered in public. It was her husband who struggled to keep his emotions under control.

Following the birthday party it seemed as though it was Bec wrestling with the demons while Ross got on with it as best he could. Bec broke down. She told him to get off the grog. Throughout her life she had always been able to go to her mother when she was looking for a shoulder to cry on. Failing that, she had close friends and family to act as confessors. But after Black Saturday there were more people looking for shoulders than providing them.

Only the Buchanans' counsellor, Annie, offered a sympathetic ear while expecting nothing in return. Bec needed Ross to get it together.

Jen and Bec, mother and daughter in July 2009. (Pic: Herald Sun.)

The funerals

The car park was overflowing and vehicles lined up for half a kilometre along both sides of Diamond Creek Road in Plenty, an outer northern suburb of Melbourne. The media were asked to stay away. Motorists drove past wondering what all the fuss was about.

Inside the Baptist Church two coffins, one which was pink and not full size and the other one blue, took up only a small space but their presence dominated the cavernous room.

As Cameron stared at the coffins he wanted very badly to remember Macca and Neeve as smiling and vibrant children brimming with the joy of their own existence.

Instead the images that came to him were from Number One Reserve Road on February 8. Images that had left him struggling for breath. A lump in his throat grew bigger and bigger, and the service hadn't begun.

Still, he thought, it could have been worse. He looked over at Ross and Bec.

It was April 27, just six days after Danny's funeral. The family felt they had been ushered out of that particular service at Whittlesea too quickly and even though a government agency funded the funerals of the fire victims, they believed it was crucial that their grieving be allowed to run its natural course. They needed to take more ownership of the services.

Hundreds of friends and family crowded into the church, and then hundreds more filled the anteroom. When that was also full people stood outside. More than a thousand people came to say goodbye, and every person at the funeral had something in common.

Deep inside they wanted to somehow come to terms with the deaths of two human beings who had perished before they'd even really set out on the great journey of life. Macca was just finding his way to the starting line. Neeve? A guileless young spirit, she epitomised all that's innocent about the human experience. It simply wasn't fair. But saying that suggests there's a God or a Great Arbiter in the Sky who dishes out doses of fairness to some families and withholds it from others. It doesn't make sense so best not even to think about it.

Just shut it out, like Cameron was shutting out the images of what he'd seen at Reserve Road.

Calum and Aiden took part in the service, friends and relatives spoke and everyone cried.

Most poignant of all were the videos and pictures of the children, so very much alive barely ten weeks earlier. Children sobbed and adults wanted to reach out and hug them and tell them it would all be OK, but again "words" fell short of corralling feelings.

Ross had organised twenty-one drummers to offer a salute to the two young drummers who had perished. Neeve's music teacher, John Cameron, wrote the score and one of the drummers, Macca's friend Blake, contributed to the salute and then joined another mate on guitar to sing a song.

It was a considerable achievement by people so young.

As the funeral came to an end Macca and Neeve's friends tagged the caskets in a final goodbye. It was Calum's idea. A shop in Dandenong also donated some colourful stick-on beads which were given out to the children. They came forward and attached them to the coffin of the nine-year-old. It was so unbearably sad that some had to turn away.

People shuffled respectfully out of the church feeling numb and hardly knowing what to say.

Ross Buchanan on the song he performed at the funerals – "Beautiful Creation"

The song "Beautiful Creation" was written in 2008 with the help of Neeve whilst sitting on our veranda out the back. Many hours together were spent on our veranda doing songs and pretending to be rock stars and the national park was our audience. It was at a time when I was in the shit with Bec and the song was dedicated to her. It was written over a couple weeks after we noticed a pigeon that would walk from our back yard to the front yard every morning and every evening, as if almost like clockwork, without a worry in the world. The pigeon has flown. I played "Beautiful Creation" at Kinglake's last open mike for the year in December 2008 with Neeve on vocals, Macca on drums and Aiden on keyboards. A proud moment indeed.

I sang "Beautiful Creation" at the kids' funeral after saying the following –

On February 7th 2009 Mother Nature was given the opportunity to attack and she took the life of two of her greatest fans. Mother Nature, I forgive you."

"Beautiful Creation" by Ross and Neeve Buchanan:

THINKING ABOUT THE LESSONS TO BE LEARNED

WHERE WE ARE AT THIS POINT WHICH WAY DO I TURN

HOW'D IT ALL GO WRONG

I'M HEARING WHAT YOU SAY

JUST MOVING RIGHT ALONG

LIVING FOR ANOTHER DAY

WHAT'S BEEN DONE CAN'T BE UNWOUND ITS HISTORY AND OUR PAST

DON'T LOOK BACK YOU'LL JUST RECALL WHAT SLIPPED THROUGH YOUR GRASP

BEAUTIFUL CREATION

PLEASE WHY DON'T YOU STAY

BEAUTIFUL CREATION

DON'T YOU FLY AWAY

BEAUTIFUL CREATION

PLEASE WHY DON'T YOU STAY

BEAUTIFUL CREATION

DON'T YOU FLY AWAY

IT'S NOT ABOUT WHO WAS WRONG AND WHO WAS RIGHT

WORK IT OUT THROUGH THE TUNNEL INTO THE LIGHT

BEAUTIFUL CREATION

PLEASE WHY DON'T YOU STAY

BEAUTIFUL CREATION

DON'T YOU FLY AWAY

THINKING ABOUT THE LESSONS TO BE LEARNED

You can pay for a funeral but what price a life?

The vast majority of bushfire funds went to individuals and communities to help them recover materially. But what of the bereaved families? How do you compensate a family for the loss of a loved one? Is there an appropriate allocation of donated or government dollars which should go to a family that's been tragically ripped asunder by death in the disaster? Are there times when money is irrelevant?

This is an extract from an email Ross and Bec sent to Prime Minister Rudd and others after the Buchanans appeared on the TV program *60 Minutes*.

Some of the questions that we are continually asked, including on the web chat after the *60 Minutes* program, are –

Are you happy with the way the Red Cross is distributing the money?

If people are receiving $50,000 for losing a house what has your family received for losing two children and a brother?

At this stage people in our situation have received a $15,000 funeral payment per death. A $10,000 payment from TAC that went direct to funeral homes. For families in our situation is this the final payment for the loss of our loved ones? This figure to us personally is like we are being told Danny, Macca and Neeve are not even worth the equivalent of one house! Our psychologist and our family doctors are working with us to re-enter the workforce, however this will take a long time. Even our one appointment with a "Business Mentor" basically concluded that 40% of my business potential burnt down (existing houses). Any new houses eventually being built, in most cases, will have their pump supply and installation organised by their building company as a package deal. This is something we would never be able to compete with. Many houses still standing received new pumps donated from various organisations. We also lost many regular customers due to loss of life or to leaving the mountain permanently. My wife's part time job, to make ends meet, at Kinglake Hardware and Produce Store is still unavailable. We are living in our house with my two remaining children Calum (18) and Aiden (13) and Calum's long term girlfriend, Lauren (18). You may also be aware of and even met with Rebecca's father and mother, Mick and Jenny Clark, who are also residing with us. Can you imagine what it is like walking past Neeve and Macca's empty bedrooms everyday? There are individuals and businesses that are actually better placed because of the fires but we will never ever be even close to that situation.

Part of the response from VBRRA chair Christine Nixon –

Ross, you highlight the specific payments made to those who have lost family to date, being the Victorian Bushfire Appeal Fund Compassion and Bereavement payment, and the Transport Accident Commission Bushfire Funeral Expense payment. As you note, these payments are primarily for meeting costs, rather than acknowledging the loss you have experienced. They are not considered by us to meet a 'value' for your loss, as this would be impossible. Having said this, the Appeal Fund Advisory Panel continues to meet very regularly, and people under distress and in hardship continue to be a subject of focus for us. We will take up for discussion your point about support for those families specifically affected by the loss of loved ones.

In November 2009 VBRRA announced it was increasing the size of its payment to bereaved families.

CHAPTER 16

MORE MONEY MATTERS

REPORTERS WANTING TO cover stories at the football club asked behind the scenes to speak to someone who'd lost a house. That was the theme throughout the football/netball season. Photographers wanted to take pictures of players who suffered losses, journalists wanted to interview them.

At first the players were hesitant but as the season wore on they became media pros. They were comfortable with the questions and knew what the photographers and cameramen wanted.

A couple of months after the fires the heavy lifters arrived. *60 Minutes* wanted to do a story. Producers were chasing the Buchanans and realised the club could help. Ross wasn't interested in further media coverage, unless there was payment involved. He desperately wanted to find enough dollars so Bec wouldn't be under pressure to work. It seemed unreasonable that she'd been through extreme trauma but should be expected to cope with the daily workplace grind. Ross was also upset that money was flying around like chaff during a hay harvest but it wasn't always going to the right people.

The federal government had made $1,000 payments available to people who had been injured, hospitalised or lost homes during the fires. More money was of course available later to those who had suffered substantial losses, but those initial payments were made to help out during the post-fire emergency.

Because so many had lost everything in the disaster no identification was required when applying for the $1,000 handout. The state government also handed out an identical amount to people who had "evacuated" during the fires.

In the Yarra Valley some families were "double or triple dipping". One family member would claim the $1,000 evacuation money, ostensibly to stay in a motel for a few nights, and then other family members would make the same claim.

In the nearby Dandenong Ranges teenagers who had left home because of a fire in the general region spent their $1,000 at the Knox City shopping centre. One young woman used the evacuation money to pay her car insurance, while a young guy, who happened to be staying at his girlfriend's house during a Dandenong Ranges fire, used the money for a Queensland holiday.

Pat McNamara, a former politician who sat on the Victorian Bushfire Appeal Fund committee, said they expected to hand over about $2 million. But the final tally was $67 million and he wanted to know who the 67,000 people were who claimed that money.

Both governments were caught in a bind; it was better to pay out the money to everyone, including people who were rorting the system, than to risk not paying one single disaster victim.

Under the circumstances Ross had no misgivings about asking Channel Nine for money. Producer Phil Goyen was sympathetic to the Buchanans' plight but said there was a general public misconception that *60 Minutes* shelled out huge sums of money. In the end they settled on an amount that barely made it into five figures.

Ross was also keen to help the football club. After the program went to air the Buchanans made themselves available for the web chat on the Channel Nine site when people asked them about their financial situation. The Channel Nine site also published KFNC's web address.

More Money Matters

The footy club had agreed to market Ross's CD *Pay Dirt* on its site. He sold two copies.

∽

During the production of the *60 Minutes* story veteran reporter Charles Wooley stood outside the Kinglake football club pavilion and watched the players train. He chatted amiably with locals and said the bushfire stories were as harrowing as any that he'd covered. People nodded knowingly. They were aware of many horrendous Black Saturday stories, not just the tragic fate of the Buchanan children.

However, they mostly weren't aware of the Darrin Gibson story that shared time with the Buchanans when the *60 Minutes* program went to air four months after the fires. Some couldn't bring themselves to watch it, others were rendered speechless.

Darrin Gibson was armed only with a hose as the fire raced across a wheat field towards his home in Coombs Road, not far from the Naylors.

There had been no warning about the impending doom, nothing on the internet or radio, until minutes before the fire arrived at Kinglake West. He immediately ran to the front fence to check on the smoke and was shaken to see fire already bearing down on the property along a front so wide he couldn't see where it ended.

The former soldier, who had served in the Solomon Islands and Iraq, had come with wife Lesley and their three children to live in their patch of paradise among the gum trees just seven months earlier.

Paradise was turning into purgatory; it was hopeless trying to battle the flames and Darrin retreated inside the house. The building caught fire within minutes.

It was their only shelter from the flames but as the house began burning the smoke turned toxic. Darrin had trouble breathing and yelled at his family to "get out". He carried one-year-old Ava and took three-year-old Jye with him. Lesley carried four-year-old Kiona.

Once outside the radiant heat was almost unbearable. Lesley yelled out, "It's burning, it's burning", and Darrin told her to get over the fence and run for the dam, just twenty metres further down the hill. Somehow Lesley and Kiona clambered over but then she just sat on the burning ground cradling her daughter. Darrin urged her to get up and head for the dam. Flames were all around them.

Lesley said, "I can't move." Her daughter was still in her arms.

Darrin quickly summed up his options and decided his priority was to see Ava to safety then come back for the others. He placed Jye on a towel on the ground and ran to the dam with one-year-old Ava. There was a small fence around the dam and he threw Ava over it to what he hoped was the edge of the water.

Darrin's shoes melted away and he was in agony every time his feet hit the scorching ground. He raced back to where he thought he'd left Jye, but he couldn't find his son in the smoke. Screaming in pain with every step Darrin then ran to Lesley and Kiona. They were both dead. Again he ran down to the dam and grabbed Ava.

They lay in the water with only their heads exposed to the heat. Ava's eyes were closed and her skin was peeling off, but she was talking. She was calling for "Mum". Darrin and Ava survived. The rest of his family perished.

He spent a month in a coma in the Alfred Hospital burns unit with Jenny Clark. Darrin's feet were so badly burnt his toes were amputated.

When he awoke from the induced coma he learned that Ava's life support machine had been turned off three days after they had been admitted to hospital.

Bec Buchanan revealed on *60 Minutes* that she'd been talking with her children some weeks before the fires about what she would do if one of them died. She said she'd probably curl up and die as well. But now here she was, two of her children were gone and she was still standing. Sometimes she wished she'd been in the house with them. The *60 Minutes* crew spent more than three days with the Buchanans; at times the interviewing process was traumatic.

At one stage Mick Clark, a normally genial bloke in his 70s, took exception to the way his daughter and wife were being interviewed and also to things he thought should be included in the story.

He produced a tyre lever from his caravan and was preparing to threaten the crew. Calum was in the background urging on his grandfather. Eventually he put the tyre lever away.

Ross and Bec were given barely three minutes on air but such is the influence of a national TV current affairs show that Bec was soon asked to meet with officials from the Bushfires Royal Commission.

She spent time in an office with two women, who finished up in tears. Bec also gave them another copy of her original police statement. They asked her to appear before the Royal Commission in 2010. Bec declined.

❦

Cameron Caine was throwing himself into football and the club's Bushfire Appeal Fund. In its first round of grants the club gave away more than $50,000 to local schools and emergency services. Compared to what had been lost it was barely a spark in a conflagration, but as a morale booster for the community it was a winner.

The footy world itself wasn't so sure and some local league executives were concerned the Kinglake club was "giving away its future".

Kinglake committee members offered a poignant rejoinder. They said when dozens of people you know have lost their lives, and more than 1,200 buildings have been destroyed in the Kinglake and Whittlesea areas, then some things are more important than sport.

Money kept rolling in from unlikely sources. A couple travelled down from the central Queensland coast carrying an envelope that was stuffed with more than $1,000 donated by a local footy club.

The donations were as varied in their sources as they were in the amounts – a National Party MP in New South Wales ($10,000), Calgary Kookaburras Women's Football Club, Canada ($700.03), NAB bank ($10,000), Hackham Sports Club, Adelaide ($500), a bunch of musicians from somewhere in central New South Wales ($7,000), a Rosebud pensioner who had a beer at the National Park Hotel and left behind a cheque ($1,000) and a Noble Park woman who had recently lost her brother in an incident unrelated to the fires.

That woman, Carol Bradley, was with friends and family at her brother's funeral service when they decided something positive should come from the death. She raised more than $4,000 at cake stalls and barbecues. Carol had a sporting background and wanted to give the money to the footy club and not the bushfire appeal. It went towards a scoreboard revamp.

Boxes of donated goods also kept arriving at the club. An elderly woman in New South Wales crocheted two dozen beanies, someone in Queensland sent down two bags of kids green rugby league shorts (the colour was right but the rugby league cut-off design, with shorts that sit high up the leg, was not a winner with the young footy boys), and there were water bottles and football boots and second-hand footy jumpers and netball tops.

AFL clubs kept helping. Melbourne had been there from the start and Geelong offered part of its NAB Cup winnings. St Kilda, Collingwood and Essendon were also particularly generous.

Later in the season the AFL feted Cameron with an MCG appearance on Grand Final day. He and three captains from other towns affected by the bushfires paraded on the ground carrying the Premiership Cup.

Ross Buchanan was also continually surprised at the outpouring of nationwide generosity and goodwill. His eleven-year-old niece Genna helped organise a fundraising concert in Mansfield, at the gateway to the Victorian High Country. Traditionally the Buchanans would head to Mansfield every Easter to spend time with relatives. This year Genna decided to do something extra special to mark the passing of Macca and Neeve. She approached leading musos, and good mates of her uncle Danny, Ash Grunwald and Lloyd Spiegel, to perform. They generously obliged.

Other artists, including Ross's Pay Dirt band, also turned up at the concert and helped the primary school girl raise $15,000, which she gave to her Kinglake relatives.

The face of Australia may continually be evolving but the size of the heart continues to grow.

CHAPTER 17

THE SLIPPERY SLOPE

ON THE PLAYING fields the Kinglake footballers were in sensational form, winning their first three games then dropping two. They weren't beaten again before the finals and the club's high profile in the struggling community led to strong media coverage.

People who had never been to Kinglake, who wouldn't have known what Kinglake was if it fell out of the sky and landed in their backyard, began following the Lakers. Aussie Rules clubs in North America, Sweden and throughout Australia wrote or phoned to wish the Lakers all the best.

Channel Seven's *Game Day* program on Sunday mornings adopted the Lakers as their team and gave out the scores each week along with the AFL results. Cameron "Speedy" Caine, as they called him, became their favourite player as he kicked bags of goals and pushed up into second place on the League Reserve's goal kicking list.

In a great example of Aussie ironical humour Cam was branded "Speedy" because he was the slowest boy between wickets when he began playing junior cricket. That trait didn't disappear when he began playing football.

One woman in her sixties told Cam that she detested football but checked the results each week simply to see if things were running well for the Lakers. There was a fairytale season brewing at the footy and netball club.

Off the field Speedy still had the brakes on. Cam was so tense he was brittle. During one match at Kinglake the club president screamed from the boundary line that the field umpire was a "cheat".

Some club members were shocked. So was the umpire, who went over to Cameron at three quarter time and demanded a written apology. Failing that, it was possible Cam would be suspended in an outcome that would have been embarrassing for the club and the community. The president duly apologised.

He also went through with his decision to stand down from police duty after the funerals of Neeve and Macca. Cam needed some time off. Nancy made sure he took stress leave.

Since he was a youngster his ideal job had been to work as a local ranger or police officer. Now as an adult he was a country cop working ten minutes from his family home, it was about as good as he expected life to get. But as the family sat watching TV one night Cameron had his first misgivings about his career. A police training show was on the screen and the young officers were confronted by an angry man while answering a call to a domestic dispute.

Cameron's stomach knotted up and he had to leave the room. He was uncertain if he'd ever be able to deal with violence again.

Ross was sorting through issues that were just as profound. After a social function at the footy clubrooms Cam and Ross sat outside by themselves. The oval floodlights were on and the blackened trees swayed in the wind like ghostly sentinels. Few words were exchanged between the pair; they had shared so much in the previous months it was now enough to simply be there for each other.

After a long silence Cam tapped Ross on the knee and said "thanks". They went back to the Caines' house and sat outside. It was after 3 A.M. Ross began opening up.

Anger, depression and sorrow spilled out of him. His two children dead, his township destroyed. No work and little money despite the hundreds of millions of dollars being pumped into the area. It had all been welling up inside. Ross stood in the middle of the lawn and surrendered to his emotions. He opened up his arms and screamed "Fuuuuck!" as loudly as he could. It was the quintessential cry for help.

Things were so bad he changed his mind about rejecting antidepressant tablets. By August his life was collapsing. Ross couldn't work, take walks or even play the guitar, and he was turning his back on much that had sustained him.

But while the medication helped Cameron the pills only brought more misery to Ross. They gave him diarrhoea and destroyed the remnants of his sex life. In short, the antidepressants made him more depressed than ever. He gave them up and continued with his alcohol self-medication.

The middle of winter was probably the bleakest time for the community. Snow came; it was desperately cold in the caravans and tents. Areas denuded of vegetation turned to mud and slush.

Trucks and clean-up vehicles dominated the roads. Tempers frayed among those who had crammed in with relatives and friends. More people were depressed. Psychologists warn that communities need to "bottom out" after a disaster before they can start climbing their way back up the slippery slope of recovery.

Down the hill in the suburbs, from Whittlesea to Eltham and across to Lilydale, life had returned to normal in towns on the edges of the disaster zones.

Ross and Bec were invited to join the saddest club in the world called the "I Have Buried Loved Ones Club". It offered a chance for bereaving survivors to spend time together. The first meeting was scheduled for the local pub in a decision that sent Ross rushing to his Hotmail account again. He had issue" with the pub owners, and they were on Ross's hit list along with the media, the shire council and sundry others. Mostly though he thought it was inappropriate for a group of mourning parents to meet at a pub. He fired off the missives and had a small win: the venue was changed.

Emotional problems emerged in unexpected areas as well.

Cam took his eldest son Angus on a tour of the Kinglake ridge pointing out the homes he'd visited and the actions he'd taken during February 7 and 8. The tour stemmed from a chat Cam and Laura had with a counsellor at Kinglake West School. Angus and Harry seemed to be continually at each other and the aggressive attitudes spilled over into the school playground. The boys were normally robust and outgoing, but not aggressive. The counsellor told Cam his eldest son needed some "dad time", so they gave Angus a day off school.

Cam and Angus drove to the Kinglake West CFA and parked in the driveway. Cam explained that he was going to show him "why Dad was off work and why he was a bit grumpy of late". The Pheasant Creek store site was their next stop as they spent four precious hours together.

Cameron drove down streets he hadn't wanted to visit for weeks and saw the remains of some houses he'd only seen in nightmares since February 8. He told his little mate as much as he could about each ruin they drove past. When his ten-year-old son wanted to know more details, Cameron was expansive. Angus remained calm in a big eyed sort of way.

Cam will forever recall the time the pair of them spent together as the day he realised his young bloke had matured into a boy capable of holding conversations and understanding adult concepts. It was a learning time for both of them, and it made them a bit calmer.

In the Buchanan household Calum began playing soccer for Eltham again while Aiden pulled on a black and yellow footy jumper at Yea because Kinglake was unable to raise junior teams. Aiden stood out in the Under 14 competition and made the inter-league team. Eventually he came runner-up in the Yea "best and fairest" count, despite missing at least four matches. "The kid can play," Ross concluded.

Like passionate parents everywhere Ross and Bec derived great satisfaction from watching their children on the sporting fields. However, in their case there was an emotional price to pay. Black Saturday had touched so many people in Victoria that it was still a major topic of conversation months after the event. As soon as other parents realised the Buchanans were from Kinglake they were invariably asked, "did your house survive?"

When Ross answered "Yes, it did", they would say "Gees, you were lucky!"

Ross always knew from the start of the "fire question" where the thread of that particular conversation would take them. What could he do? He was a naturally gregarious person so he didn't want to avoid people, but he couldn't lie because the truth was so precious to him.

He gave the answer straight: "Yep. Lucky. The house survived but I lost a couple of children, a brother-in-law and a business."

"I'm so sorry," was the inevitable, and unfortunate, reply. There endeth the conversation.

From the Bushfires Royal Commission

The impact of disaster is felt by people in the short, medium and long term. In the short term (days to weeks) people have to focus on immediate physical and material needs, but they may have difficulties with thinking, planning and decision making. In the medium term (weeks to months) people may experience a wide range of emotions and strong feelings. They are often emotional and traumatised, or in constant distress, which can affect health and relationships. They also tend to be involved in more accidents. In the longer term (months to years) the effects of disaster can become apparent as financial consequences, health, emotional wellbeing, and other aspects of life that may have been postponed due to earlier demands, come to the fore.

While Cam and Ross recognised the benefits of talking with counsellors, of taking their problems and turning them over beneath a bright light so they could be seen from many different angles, lots of men were stoically refusing to open up. The women were different. They were more inclined to talk about the things that troubled them.

One of Cam's male friends wasn't coping well. He was having trouble sleeping at night and his waking moments were punctuated by Black Saturday recollections. A woman had died in front of him. In a final desperate plea she had urged him to take care of her children, but the two youngsters were already dead on the back seat of her car.

Cam decided that during the long cold winter the footy club needed to do something to help. Ross had also noticed the tendency of the men to "bottle it up", although it wasn't always their fault. Ross wasn't offered any counselling until weeks after the fires and it only came following a phone call from the ABC's Libbi Gorr, who was so disturbed by her interview and conversation with him that she found some professionals for him to talk to.

Ross and Cam, with some help from Wally, were put in touch with Bali bombing victim and former AFL star Jason McCartney. Jason agreed to waive his normal speaking fee for the Kinglake talk. The club put on a pie and chips meal for the community and packed out its rooms. McCartney, who played for Collingwood, Adelaide and North Melbourne, had the audience's respect before he even took the stage.

He told them how he had suffered second-degree burns to 50% of his body but had focused on helping people immediately after the Sari nightclub bombing because he didn't realise how badly he'd been injured himself. He also gave up his place on one of the early planes to leave Bali because he thought people with worse burns deserved priority treatment.

When he eventually returned to Australia he almost died on the operating table.

McCartney then focused on his recovery and the gruelling return to elite sport, which culminated in North Melbourne's momentous win over Richmond in 2003 and his subsequent retirement.

It was a gripping story iced by his confession that he was still learning to cope with the traumatic bombing seven long years later.

He urged people to seek help, not to let their problems gnaw away deep inside like a virulent disease. McCartney's credibility was so strong he could have told the Kinglakers "black was white" and they would have believed him.

The former footy star did more talks in the area and also returned to speak to the Kinglake Cricket Club later in the year.

People related to him because of his sporting background but also because he'd been through similar experiences. They were willing to listen, and learn. Most importantly, more people were willing to seek help.

⁂

Greg Norman and Chris Evert also generously gave their time to some fundraising, but their focus was on offering support to the Marysville community.

Of course, organisers looking to hook the Shark up with some bushfire victims simply went to "B for Black Saturday/Buchanan" in their contact list.

Aiden was asked to take part in a photo shoot for the Marysville Golf Club, which was playing a role in helping that beleaguered community fight back after it was wiped out by the Murrindindi fire. Never mind that Aiden doesn't play golf and, as he told Norman with characteristic confidence, doesn't even like the game. Never mind that he lives at Kinglake West, which is about 100 kilometres by mountainous road from Marysville. He was just bushfire fodder, but it was for a good cause.

Bec presented Evert and Norman with pink ribbons emblazoned in black with the names of Neeve and Macca. Ross gave them some footy club merchandise, including caps and wristbands.

They politely accepted the gifts but Evert was surprised when Bec told her the visit by the sporting superstars wouldn't help the Buchanan family one iota, although she and Ross were more than happy to support any cause that was aiding the bushfire communities.

Chrissie Evert offered to stay in touch, but the Buchanans never heard from her again and within four months the famous made in heaven marriage to Norman was over.

Ross's media cynicism reached new heights when a reporter took footage of Norman's departing aircraft, despite the Shark expressly asking them not to film the private jet.

That cynicism became further entrenched towards the end of the year when a journalist contacted the Buchanans claiming Shane Warne wanted to be photographed with Aiden. When Bec contacted Shane, he was at Los Angeles airport coming home for Christmas with his family. Shane said the journo had told *him* Aiden wanted to do a photo shoot!

It was as if the media had co-opted the Buchanans into "celebrity land" and gave barely a thought to the raw emotions that coursed through their psyches just below the surface.

CHAPTER 18

SOME MUCH-NEEDED TRACTION

Footy finals in Victoria reach deep into the public consciousness.

They bring immense pleasure to millions of people who share an interest in the unique code of football called Aussie Rules. Finals time also heralds the arrival of spring and a warmer sun. Lawns have to be mowed, lighter clothes retrieved from the back of the wardrobe and, in some well-oiled households, planning starts for Christmas.

More than just a change of seasons, it also marks a change of attitude. People become outdoors oriented and more outgoing.

It was around early spring that Cameron and Ross began to talk more about the future, although of course Ross was still drinking heavily.

Cameron discovered someone at Kinglake West CFA had nominated him for an Australian of the Year Award. Weeks later the *Herald Sun* newspaper named him as one of the ten most influential Victorians in 2009. He also went back to work, just four hours a day in the Wallan Police Station. As is standard Victoria Police procedure, Cam was told not to wear a sidearm.

Ross, Wally and others were speaking to experts about offering their own counselling to future disaster victims. Ross was also in a buoyant enough mood to play one of the great practical jokes of Victorian community football.

During Kinglake's first final against Seville, Ross led a ground invasion after the Laker full forward kicked his 100th goal for the season. Ross was then bemused when commentators on the local community radio station remarked about the "big bums" on the Laker players. They were said to be too old and too fat to have much impact on the finals series.

Kinglake came from six goals down to win by six against Seville. Ross was on a roll; he spent $300 on "big plastic bums" which he and Cam sprayed in green and gold, the club colours, and gave out to supporters. Laker fans later wore the big bums proudly at the Grand Final and made a point of parading past the commentary van. Ross also let the players into his private world. He brought a copy of the Libbi Gorr interview up to the pavilion and played it to the fifty senior footballers involved in the Senior and Reserves finals campaigns.

The young men were emotionally mugged by the sensitive interview and some were in tears. To a man they avoided eye contact with him. Ross told them the moment wasn't about him, or the Black Saturday victims, it was about what the whole community had been through and how inspirational the footballers had been.

The Lakers steamrolled their way into the 2009 Grand Final of the Yarra Valley Mountain District Football League with another big win over Seville. However, they were underdogs against the powerful Olinda Ferny Creek side, which had beaten them by four goals in a semifinal.

In the meantime, the metropolitan media were back on board talking about the Lakers' fairytale year. Prime Minister Kevin Rudd, who agreed during the season to be the Lakers' patron, flew down from Canberra for the match, and Jimmy Stynes also said he was attending, just two days after being released from hospital.

Cameron Caine was asked to chaperone them and the PM went into both change rooms and spoke to the players. In the Lakers' rooms he gave the boys a bit of a pep talk, telling them they were an inspiration to the nation. Players are invariably told to keep to a normal routine prior to big games, but having a change room audience with the PM is about as abnormal as a post-season trip to Greenland!

Back outside again Mr Rudd grabbed a VB beer, the green can, the working man's beer, and proceeded to spend the next four hours mingling with the crowd and posing for photographs while he sipped the drink. At the end of the match he was in the middle of the Kinglake player huddle, fans didn't realise it was the PM until they pushed to the front so they could see the footballers. But he declined all media interviews because he said the day was about the players and the Kinglake people, not about him.

Cam was the perfect host in his colourful green and yellow hat. He smiled as he introduced the nation's leader and Jimmy Stynes to people. He posed for photographs with them individually and as a trio, and he also completed interviews with the three commercial TV networks. It was the biggest day in the century-long history of the Kinglake footy club, and it couldn't have happened without Cameron and Laura Caine.

More than that, it was a wonderful day for the Kinglake community. An estimated five thousand people attended the game. The Lakers fans were decked out in club colours and greeted each other with hugs and huge smiles.

They had come to see their team in action, a group of young men who represented a township that had borne the brunt of the worst natural disaster in Australian history.

Ross agreed to sing the national anthem again. He also agreed to talk to the media, who were eager to portray the day as an occasion for celebration and "moving on". Ross, as usual, had his own agenda. He'd talk about things that would help him move on, but he was still deeply mired in a battle with the outside world for some pecuniary justice to compensate for the family's losses. There were also a host of other issues that needed raising.

He had laboured over that A4-sized sheet of issues he intended to present to the media, but of course when the time came to face the cameras the journos only wanted to know one thing: "how he felt."

Ross Buchanan, "Lakers fan who lost two children on Black Saturday", went to air on the TV news that night in a fifteen second grab thanking the club for helping the community to recover. If you look closely at that clip his soulless eyes tell a different story, they show a man still deeply troubled by emotions and memories bottled up inside him. A man who believes the real Ross Buchanan died on February 7, 2009, in a house in Reserve Road, Kinglake.

All the tears and the anger couldn't help the old Ross Buchanan return. Nor could they erase the precious memories his mind returned to every single day, like a hot and tired man returning to a cool, sweet stream that flows a bit slower on each visit.

After the TV interviews at the grand final Ross disappeared upstairs into the pavilion to escape other media. Then when the time came to sing the national anthem, unaccompanied and in front of the prime minister and the assembled players, Ross was missing.

Was it possible that during the seven and a half months since the fires he'd taken on board so much ballast it had finally sunk him? That he'd fought so many battles with various agencies and the media and wrestled so often with his own demons that he'd finally lost the war?

Perhaps he was sobbing uncontrollably somewhere in a quiet room upstairs, or even worse, perhaps his own "upstairs room" had given up on the future?

Organisers put a recorded version of the national anthem on standby; one of them anxiously asked Bec if Ross was OK. She said simply, "He'll be here." And he was.

The crowd was about eight deep in front of the main gate and Ross pushed his way through and out on to the ground where he bravely took the microphone. Ross told the PM and five thousand fans that they needed to join in and help him. He gave them about as rusty a rendition of the anthem as you would hear sober. But no one cared; it was about "the moment", not the tune.

People joined in with such alacrity that fans on the far side of the oval said they couldn't even hear Ross because the singing was so loud. For the thousands of Kinglake people wearing their green and gold it was a moment they would never forget. Ross was their bloke and he was leading them through it.

When he was finished, balloons were released for the Black Saturday victims. There was one pink balloon for Neeve and a blue one for Macca. Ross then collapsed into Bec's arms. Despite everything they had been through since February, incredibly, it was the first time they had hugged in front of the cameras.

Thousands of people watched, and thousands of hearts reached out to them across a space that couldn't be bridged.

Football legend Jim Stynes, who was battling cancer, Prime Minister Kevin Rudd and Cam at the Kinglake v Olinda Ferny Creek Grand Final. (Pic: Craig Sillitoe, Fairfax.)

The Caine and Buchanan families. Left to right from rear: Laura, Cameron, Calum, Sian, Rebecca, Ross, Lauren (Calum's girlfriend), Aiden, Angus and Harry on the bottom right. This pic was taken a month before the first anniversary of Black Saturday. (Pic: family collection.)

PART TWO

CHAPTER 1

A STROLL IN THE GARDEN

CAMERON CAINE'S LIFE changed remarkably after the Lakers played in the grand final. The match was extensively covered by the media because it was one of the few feel-good stories to emerge post-Black Saturday.

At the same time, after a harrowing year, Cam began to think of his career options. He was content working as a police officer just ten minutes from home and playing footy with his mates. But could he do better for his family? Could he provide them with more opportunities and choices?

Coincidently, Dave Brooks and his music comedy show, the Musicmen, performed at the footy club and Brooksy offered to put Cam in touch with someone on the public speaking circuit.

Cam and Ross spoke at length about sharing their experiences with a public audience and decided to take it further. Ross wasn't sure if he was emotionally equipped to talk publicly about those issues he knew people would demand to hear. But he shared his mate's belief that he was obliged to do the best he could for his family.

The speaking agency they were referred to was keen to get Cam on board, but less so Ross because he sounded, and looked, a bit erratic. Extraordinarily, it wasn't until towards the end of their first chat with the agency "suit" that the executive realised Ross had actually lost loved ones in the fires. That was a game changer.

Perhaps because of his entertainment background Ross took to the speaking circuit like a kid on an Easter egg hunt. Cam said Ross was blowing them away, although he had to remind his mate not to push personal agendas that would alienate an audience unfamiliar with the aftermath of the fire.

People still wanted to hear what they'd always wanted to hear – "How did you feel?" But of course, they were also interested to learn "How do you feel now?"

The truth was Ross had gone from feeling like his life was over to wanting to find some way to cope with the new realities. In contrast, Cam's life was about to head off on a tangent as exciting as it was unforseen, and as challenging as it was replete with opportunities.

Towards the end of 2009 Cam and Laura attended the Australian of the Year "Local Hero" awards. He didn't win it, that honour went to a couple who volunteered their time to rebuild fences destroyed on Black Saturday, but this is the way organisers summed up Cam's contribution to the Kinglake community –

"Constable Cameron Caine has always been an integral member of the Kinglake Ranges community but during the Black Saturday fires, he helped save the lives of many individuals. However, it was in the days following the fires that his community spirit really shone. Cameron had the unenviable task of discovering the deceased, many of whom he knew personally, and informing family and friends. Cameron is President of the Kinglake Football and Netball Club and saw this as an opportunity to help the community regain its spirit.

"The club was physically and emotionally devastated by the fires but Cameron's leadership refocused the club members who then rallied along with the wider community to reform in time to play the first football match of the 2009 season, which they won. Cameron rebuilt the spirit of the club and together they raised $130,000 to help the community recover."

Of course, the club actually raised about $180,000 but the money, once it was spread among so many community groups, was probably not as important as the role that KFNC had played as a social and recreational focal point for people post-bushfires.

Cameron was embarrassed to be singled out for the award, partly because as a police officer he was simply doing the job he was paid to do. He also thought there were many others, particularly his partner Roger Wood, who were just as deserving, if not more so, than he was. The description of him as a hero grated with him.

But Cam's public profile was rising inexorably. After Christmas he had an opportunity to meet Prince William when he toured the bushfire regions and attended the same function as the Caines at Government House.

While clearly not as imposing as Edinburgh Castle, Melbourne's Government House, with its flag flying imperiously atop a white mansion, nevertheless casts an aura of privilege and power over the beautiful parklands on the CBD's southern edge.

Now the Caines found themselves on the inside of this world – the stomping ground of Melbourne's elites.

It was hot in the cavernous main hall and they could barely see the prince. Soon enough they were ushered outside into the garden where people stood in a long line waiting to shake the royal hand. As William approached them pint-sized Laura nudged her big husband forward and he introduced himself as "Cameron Caine, the president of the Kinglake Football Netball Club".

Cam told the prince he had a Kinglake football jumper to give him. The prince responded warmly then moved on. His aides told Cam he'd missed a chance for a one-on-one meeting earlier but if he fetched the jumper they'd make sure William received it.

William then disappeared further down the garden to plant a tree, but it seemed the Caines had made an impression on him. One of the aides confided to Cam that if he hurried he could still meet the prince and personally hand over the guernsey.

Cam, who was wearing his police uniform, raced out to grab the jumper from the car then leapt back over a fence and hurried into the garden. Meanwhile, he'd lost contact with his wife and officials were dispatched to look for "Laura from Kinglake". Quickly, she rejoined him and together they approached Prince William.

Despite everything he'd been through in the preceding eleven months Cam had never been more nervous. The prince was with Governor David de Kretser and Victorian Premier John Brumby. Cam towered over him as he presented William with the green and gold jumper. William smiled from ear to ear and said he was extremely honoured to receive the jumper which he lifted to his nose. "Is it washed, Cameron?" he asked. "You have no idea how many dirty jumpers I get handed."

Laura and Cam spoke to him for about ten minutes; William also revealed he'd had a chat to Bec Buchanan earlier in the day who, in a typically matter-of-fact Aussie manner, told him to keep his eye out for the Kinglake policeman.

The prince came across as a down-to-earth guy who was genuinely interested to hear about the role the Lakers played in bushfire recovery.

Cameron presents Prince William with a Kinglake jumper while Victorian Premier John Brumby (centre) and Governor David de Kretser (right) look on. (Pic: family collection.)

A Stroll in the Garden

Bec met Prince William in Whittlesea, but not before her husband had savaged the media pack following the royal personage. Ross was at an emotional low when he went to Whittlesea for an appointment with his psychologist. He walked into the township's hub building not knowing the prince was visiting and was ambushed by a posse of journalists. Ross went wild and demanded the media wait elsewhere, he then launched a tirade at Christine Nixon.

Nixon was caught in the middle of the verbal storm and she and Ross agreed to disagree about the rights and wrongs of what had just taken place. Ross was then taken outside for a walk to cool down.

Bec also had a meeting with the psychologist, and an impromptu audience with Prince William was organised for her. They spent ten minutes chatting privately about the fires, the recovery and her plan to head overseas to visit disaster memorials.

Murrindindi Shire had been given $600,000 to spend on a Black Saturday memorial, or memorials, and Bec had been asked to contribute ideas. Because she was starting with a blank page she decided she needed to see what had been done internationally with major memorials in terms of dollars spent, public input and the aesthetics of the various designs.

Prince William spoke to Bec about her plans and gave advice on where she might like to go and some of the memorials she should visit. His people later contacted Bec when she was in Britain and helped her locate and visit some of the UK's best known memorial sites.

A photographer from the Department of Human Services (DHS) took a picture of Bec and the prince together and *New Idea* magazine offered to help fund Bec's trip if they could run the story and the picture.

The prince's staff had no objections, but DHS initially refused to release the photo and duly incurred the wrath of Ross. A nasty email from Ross eventually persuaded DHS to agree to the picture being featured in the magazine but by then it was too late, and *New Idea* had lost interest.

In the weeks ahead Bec and Ross sent out dozens of emails trying to secure support for her overseas trip and eventually some companies came on board, as did Christine Nixon who dug into her own pocket to help.

The Buchanans, and many others in the bushfire regions, had developed personal relationships with Nixon and stood shoulder to shoulder with the former police chief when her world began to crumble at the Bushfires Royal Commission.

It would all reach a climax at a most unlikely time and place.

CHAPTER 2

MOVING ON?

Ross and Bec had people to love, and many people who loved them in return and who, with all their hearts, willed them to find some peace somewhere in life. Of course, these same people knew very well that there was no chance the Buchanans could move on completely as long as their children's memories lingered.

Bec had worked for the Global Care charity in Kinglake and later embroiled herself in the process of designing a bushfire memorial. Ross had less structure in his life; he had less to do and less to look forward to. The speaking circuit bookings only dribbled in.

However, there had been one break in the cloud cover when a pump company offered him some work in Tasmania after the football Grand Final. Because he'd lost $75,000 worth of pumps in the fires he was able to claim an insurance pay out that he and Bec lived on for much of 2009. Orange Pumps, which actually owned the equipment, never officially waived the bill but instead gave Ross an opportunity to work it off.

He headed to Tassie and toured the island, giving pump repair training with an Orange employee. It was a successful trip until Ross's companion discovered that his wife had walked out on him while he was away and he engaged Ross as a confessor figure. Ross was not the right person to be taking on extra emotional baggage.

With Christmas 2009 looming Ross began to worry that he had too much time on his hands. It would be the first Yuletide without Macca and Neeve and their deaths would be brought into razor-sharp relief. Christmas would be followed all too soon by Macca's birthday and then the anniversary of February 7.

These events had the potential to send him scurrying back down a profoundly dark hole of depression. So Ross took pre-emptive action. As well as public speaking he began to think about a project he'd started some years before. He resumed writing a play about goldminers in the Kinglake area in the nineteenth century; some of his work had already been set to music.

He called it *Pay Dirt – The Musical* and the idea of completing the project loomed ever larger in his mind until he began working on it for hours each day. Soon he began to put some more creative flesh on the bare bones of the script and became confident enough to talk with mates about it.

Ross hoped he could create something that local schools would embrace and, who knew, perhaps he could take it further. About the same time Ross, Wally and a few friends began discussing the idea of staging a music concert somewhere in the city to say "Thank you, Melbourne".

It was to be their way of acknowledging the generous input of millions of people who helped the bushfire victims. It was also to be the start of months of hard work as the small group of eager Kinglakers tried to turn an idea brimming with excitement and goodwill into a practical outcome.

The detail that is involved in taking good ideas and turning them into practical outcomes is of course the straw that has broken the back of many optimistic volunteers, as Ross and Wally were about to discover.

In the meantime, something dramatic was happening in Cam's life.

After seven years on the footy committee the local cop knew he was able to command a certain amount of respect when speaking in public, and of course he was a dedicated community worker. He was also a natural leader; locals looked to him for advice and guidance.

Cam had considered standing for local council but because of the irregular hours he worked, and the huge amount of time he devoted to the football and netball club, it was a commitment he couldn't make.

However, late in 2009 the popular local member of federal parliament, Fran Bailey, announced she was retiring. Friends suggested Cameron should consider replacing her. He initially thought the idea was absurd, what did he know about the labyrinthine world of federal politics? The House of Representatives, along with its arcane procedures and party politics, couldn't be further removed from the earthy reality of Cam's Kinglake life.

Still, he did relate well to people and he was driven by a "call to help" those less fortunate than his own family. He had spent 2009 immersed in bushfire recovery and he was eager to make sure the recovery program kept receiving the help and attention it needed. Like many others Cam feared that once the media spotlight moved on from the bushfire regions, public interest would wane and the recovery would lose its impetus. It would also mean there would be less political pressure on the various government departments to get the job done.

Already housing reconstruction had begun to lag, and at the time of the first anniversary of Black Saturday work had begun on barely one third of the homes destroyed in the bushfires.

There had also been unforseen problems. For example, people who wanted to rebuild in the most fire-prone areas had to meet strict new building guidelines. But meeting those guidelines was proving so expensive that the families couldn't afford construction costs.

John Butterworth's situation was a good example. His two boys, Adam and Jayden, played football for Kinglake. His house, on a 40-hectare block at Kinglake West, was destroyed on February 7 and John was lucky to escape with his life. Adam's house was also destroyed, as was that of their mother who had separated from John.

Because the construction of John Butterworth's house had to meet "flame zone standards" it was going to cost at least $70,000 just to put the windows in! That was more than four times the amount John had budgeted for. It was simply money he didn't have.

Although the reconstruction was administered by state and local government bodies, Cam concluded that at least he'd be closer to the powerbrokers if he was in federal parliament.

Friends also told Cam that if he was going to move on with his life it was the right time to look at career options. He wasn't so sure. The lifestyle he enjoyed, living in a country town, a great job close to home, playing football with his mates, was uncomplicated and secure.

He and Laura spent a long night talking about it. If Cam decided to go into politics, and if Fran Bailey anointed him and if he then won the seat… well, their world would be turned upside down. He'd be in Canberra ninety days a year and when he was able to sleep at home on weekends he'd be out at electorate functions on most Saturdays and Sundays. Angus, Harry and Sian would be without a dad for long periods of time.

It was a major family sacrifice; even so, after much discussion, they agreed to "give it a go".

Early in 2010 word got back to Bailey that Cameron Caine, the local cop who'd provided leadership to the Kinglake community during and after the bushfire disaster, could be interested in standing for federal parliament. Bailey had survived the Howard Government wipe out of the 2007 election when the Liberals lost office. She'd clung to her seat of McEwen by the slimmest of margins, just thirty-one votes. Having fought so hard to keep the seat in the conservative camp Bailey had no intention of seeing it move to the left after she retired. She wanted a high-profile candidate to pick up the political cudgels on her behalf.

First she approached Dean Jones, the former cricket star who lives on the western edge of the electorate. But Dean was heavily involved in cricket commentary and wasn't ready for a career change. It later emerged that the one-time "world's best batsman in limited overs cricket" also had some serious domestic issues that he had to sort his way through.

After Bailey heard that Cameron was considering a political future she turned her attention to the Kinglake copper. The pair met in Healesville. Cam was at pains to point out to the former Howard Government minister that he was not a political person. He didn't know or understand the intricacies of the various political debates that flared from time to time across the national landscape. But Bailey recognised that Cam was good with people and the previous twelve months had shown that he would make a caring and effective local member. He was one of those special people who, while he was a good listener himself, seemed to be listened to by others as well.

After a long conversation the deal was done. Bailey would persuade the local Liberals that Cam was her heir apparent and he would start work lifting his profile in the electorate and trying to ensure the seat didn't fall into Labor hands.

Ironically, some of the staunchest Labor supporters in the McEwen electorate, according to the 2007 election booth figures, were in Kinglake and Kinglake West. But Cam knew he could count on at least two local votes, his mum and dad. They had both been Liberal Party members. They had also spent a lifetime building up a local haulage company in the Diamond Creek area at the foot of the mountain and Cam could relate strongly to the small business struggles they'd been through. They had the sort of true-blue Liberal bona fides that would help Cam establish some credibility within the party.

In the meantime, Laura gave up her position as treasurer at the club; the workload was unrelenting and she was simply exhausted. Kinglake Football Netball Club turned over more than $300,000 in 2009 and that was a lot of money for Laura to keep track of!

The KFNC Bushfire Appeal also donated around $180,000 to the community, so combined it was close to a half million-dollar business that Laura had fiduciary responsibility for. At one stage she "lost" $30,000 and spent many sleepless nights worrying about why the books didn't tally. How could she lose $30,000? What would the other KFNC committee members say, indeed what would the media say? Would local police have to become involved?

It was only when she sought help from Rohan McLellan, a Kinglake player and managing director of club sponsor Promains, that Laura was able to discover where the money had gone. Rohan noticed that the new KFNC eftpos machine had been incorrectly linked to the bushfire appeal account and not the club's general account, which meant every time someone used a credit card at the bar the money was sent to the wrong account. Rohan and Laura painstakingly audited the $30,000 worth of transactions.

She had good reason to be tired!

There were also signs early in 2010 that KFNC was about to become the focus of media and public attention yet again. The footballers and netballers were invited to a prime ministerial Australia Day reception at the National Gallery where Mr Rudd met Cam in St Kilda Road and greeted him like an old mate.

Inside the Great Hall, the Kinglake people quickly availed themselves of the refreshments, but their eyes glazed over as the PM spoke for more than half an hour about the need to boost Australia's productivity rates to pay for the retirement of the Baby Boomer generation. They were quick to work out where the alcohol was coming from and stationed themselves outside that door so they had first call on the beer and wine.

They stayed until the booze ran out then disappeared into the Melbourne night.

Media heavyweight Eddie McGuire also wanted the players to visit his Triple M radio studios in early February, and there were other demands on the Lakers and their committee.

It was too much for Laura. The endless list of requests also claimed another victim when highly respected Kinglake football coach Michael Nott resigned so he could concentrate on work and family. However, Cam decided to stay on as president and simply shouldered a bigger load.

Laura then learned that her parents were planning a golden anniversary and because her father was too old to travel, they asked if there was any chance she could visit them in Scotland? She decided to take the boys and head home for a few weeks of rest and recuperation. They left just as Cam's workload exploded.

He was back at Kinglake police station, he was running a

football-netball club that was continually in the public spotlight and he was also now trying to stand for federal parliament. There was barely an afternoon or morning free in his diary for as far as he could see into the future. Not for the last time he began to wonder what he'd signed on for.

∽

Ross was similarly busy. He was writing *Pay Dirt* and working on the Thank You Melbourne free concert. Bec's friend and Whittlesea Country Music Festival coordinator, Mahony Kiely, got together with Ross and they began visiting possible concert venues. They checked out Melbourne's major venues including Federation Square, the Sidney Myer Music Bowl and the best known "sticky carpet" pub, the Corner Hotel in Richmond.

The Corner is a hotel with a beery rock music reputation. Consequently, it was deemed not suitable for children, while the other two iconic Melbourne sites were major league venues with major league organisational challenges such as crowd control and stage management. They could host tens of thousands of people.

It was a potentially immense challenge for the Kinglakers.

Another not insignificant problem was paying for the hire of the venue. Ross, Wally, Mahony and the others had decided not to apply for any of the bushfire appeal money. They agreed those dollars, which were fast running out, were better spent on people recovering from the fires.

Coincidently, Cam and Ross met Premier Brumby in Kinglake's main street and happened to mention the proposed concert to him. The Victorian leader immediately offered his personal support for the project and said he'd try to find some money to ensure it went ahead. Mr Brumby promised $35,000.

A concert similar to the one they planned had cost over $45,000 to stage at Kinglake but, to Ross's chagrin, that was partly due to a couple of the headline acts asking for $4,000 to appear. In contrast, Ross had played for forty minutes for free. He was determined the spirit of the

Thank You Melbourne concert wouldn't be hijacked by artists looking for an easy pay day.

But then they discovered it would cost $50,000 just to hire the Myer Music Bowl. They were taking half a step forward and one step backwards.

Again Ross went cap in hand to the corporates. He and Mahony also visited the Blue Ribbon Foundation, the police charity group, in search of funds. That meeting got off to a bad start when they were asked if they had lost houses in the fires.

The Blue Ribbon people told Ross and Mahony to think bigger, to consider hiring the indoor sports stadium at Docklands where 50,000 people could be seated, and to search for a headline act. Ross said they already had commitments from artists they knew personally, including Ash Grunwald, Lloyd Spiegel, Ruckus and many others from the Kinglake ridge. The Blue Ribbon people suggested they should aim for the top shelf and approach the music star John Farnham.

Ironically, within a few weeks people associated with Farnham came close to derailing the entire project.

❦

Mahony Kiely was a rock in the lives of Ross and Bec during their many times of need after the fires. She also played a crucial role in organising the Thank You Melbourne concert. At the same time as she was helping to put together the concert, she was also working on the elaborate Indigenous ceremony which preceded the Essendon-Richmond AFL match.

Ross describes her as an "amazing woman living an extraordinary life". When she was just a young woman, with twin girls, she decided to travel and headed overseas with just her two daughters and a backpack!

❦

Ross may have been heading towards unfamiliar territory, but Cam was already there. Cam had little idea how much support he'd have from

Liberals within the seat of McEwen, although he was assured by Party HQ that they would be pumping significant resources into the electorate because they were determined to hold the seat.

The Labor Party was just as determined to take the Victorian seat and compensate for any losses in the northern states. It was clear Cam would face a major fight to keep them at bay in an election that could be called as late as 2011 but would most likely be held in the second half of 2010.

Bailey's personal vote in the electorate was put at up to 3% because of the hard work she had done over the last twenty years. It would be virtually impossible for Cam to personally win the confidence of those thousands of "Fran people" before the election.

Changing demographics also presented Cam with another hurdle. The seat's population had grown markedly since Bailey scraped over the line in 2007. An extra 10,000 people now lived in McEwen and most of them had spilled over from the pro-Labor northern suburbs of Melbourne into new housing areas in the fast-growing south-west of the electorate. The trend around Mill Park, Mernda, Wallan and the other expanding suburbs would surely be pro-Labor and thus anti-Cam.

One of the few factors he had running in his favour was the dwindling popularity of the leader he was on first name terms with, Kevin Rudd. The Rudd Labor Government had begun losing significant support back in December 2009 when it shelved plans to seriously tackle climate change.

Polls were showing the government was on the nose. Labor strategists began to consider the previously unthinkable; it was becoming possible their young government could be thrown out of office after just one term. Given those problems, and Cam's strong community leadership profile, supporters felt he was surely in with a chance of winning.

However, within the electorate he was almost a "one-man forward line". Mark Beacham, the campaign manager for McEwen, was there in support but after that, Cam was, to a surprising extent, left to his own devices. That's not to say that he received no guidance from Liberal

Party headquarters. HQ was at 104 Exhibition Street in Melbourne and the Liberals commonly refer to it simply as "104". They confirmed with Cam and Mark that they would be spending hundreds of thousands of dollars in McEwen.

A handful of Liberals also attended local committee meetings, but on a day-to-day basis the senior constable was often on his own when he attended functions or went on a meet-and-greet mission. When people at these functions began to ask him questions such as "What is Liberal leader Tony Abbott going to do for the elderly," they may as well have inquired about the fate of the Galileo spacecraft. He hadn't had time to absorb the dozens of policy issues.

In contrast, his opponent was a veteran campaigner and seasoned politician. Labor's Rob Mitchell had previously sat in the Upper House of the Victorian Parliament and then stood against Fran Bailey in the 2007 federal election.

Mitchell, a former tow truck driver and truck parts salesman, had landed a job with a state government department after losing his legislative council seat in Melbourne and was already working the electorate hard. Cam viewed Mitchell as a career politicia", someone who sought to enter parliament for his own philosophical reasons while at the same time recognising it as a career with good benefits and salary.

In the mornings Mitchell was at the train stations and at night he attended various meetings. Whenever time allowed he would be door knocking and pavement pounding. While he was smooching potential supporters, Senior Constable Caine was on the police beat locking up drunks or trying to resolve domestic disputes.

Meanwhile, Greens candidate Steve Meacher also had plenty of experience and profile. He too had stood in the 2007 election and his preferences nearly tipped Mitchell into office. Meacher was a strong debater and was also up to speed on policy. He presented Cam with yet another obstacle.

Labor and the Greens eventually reached a deal to swap preferences, which meant that disillusioned Rudd supporters could put "number

1" beside the Greens on their ballot paper as a protest vote knowing full well that under the preferential system that vote would eventually flow to Labor. It meant that while they may have turned their backs on Rudd and Labor, as the polls were showing, they were still watching over their shoulders.

Cameron Caine had a tougher fight on his hands than he knew.

CHAPTER 3

TURNING BACK TIME

Just as Cam, Laura and Kinglake Football Netball Club people had been feeling the pressure of the first anniversary of Black Saturday, so too were the Buchanans under strain, especially in the lead up to a day full of trepidation that drew ever closer on the calendar.

January 31 was Macca's birthday. Memories of what had transpired twelve months earlier were still surprisingly fresh in Ross's mind. On that day in 2009 Bec was in Shepparton, in northern Victoria, promoting the Whittlesea Country Music Festival. Ross had gone along with her to MC the occasion. They'd taken Macca as well because their second oldest boy had been in a bit of trouble.

Because it was his birthday Macca was allowed to bring a mate with him, Blake. Victoria was in the midst of that 40 degree-plus mega heatwave that sucked the moisture out of the forests and gardens. They all swam in the pool and the boys were allowed to share some beers afterwards.

Ross recalls that Macca seemed proud of the way his father worked the audience as he MCed the event. Later that night Macca talked about how Chris Spezza was his best friend and would be forever. He then said he and Blake were going out to party and to soak up the Shepparton nightlife. Ross said "no way" and told him to go to bed. But Macca wasn't backing down and the disagreement soon turned into a noisy and heated confrontation. Things only cooled off when Bec intervened.

How Ross yearned for those heated arguments again with Macca!

The following day when they returned home Neeve had written "I love you" on the outside wall of their house in National Park Road. Those words were never removed and they later confronted visitors in a heart-stilling greeting.

Midway through 2010 the author went to the Buchanan house to take some photos of the boundary line where the national park presses up against the backyard. I wanted to gain a better appreciation of the height of the flames and to also record the regrowth on the trees.

Ross and Bec were out but a family friend was inside watching TV. After explaining the purpose of the visit, I took the photos and was walking back up the driveway to leave when Neeve's words of love on the front wall caught my eye.

I took some pictures in case the Buchanans wanted to include them in the book, or to simply file away for future local historians. I focused the camera and pressed the button. Nothing happened. I tried twice more, but the camera refused to operate and I gave up.

Sitting in the car outside the Buchanans' house, I checked the camera and discovered the batteries had gone flat at precisely the moment I had chosen to capture an image of probably the most unsettling message to survive Black Saturday.

Despite visiting the Buchanan house on numerous occasions, after that day I never again entertained the idea of taking a picture of Neeve's message. It lives on where it counts most, in the hearts of her parents.

After Neeve went to bed on that first Sunday in February 2009 Ross, Bec and Macca sat outside on the veranda overlooking the forest, which on that particular evening was their ally as it took the edge off the sweltering temperatures. The three of them spoke for hours. Six days later the children would be dead. Blake would later take part in the twenty-one drum salute at Macca's funeral.

So these were the thoughts that pried their way into Ross's consciousness as February 7, 2010, loomed. Oh, to turn back time.

Bec was unsure how to mark Macca's birthday so Ross had a chat to Aiden and came up with a "Skate for Macca Day" at one of the various skate parks he used to frequent. Aiden doubted they would attract many people so Ross had a $20 wager with him that if they put the idea on Facebook they would get at least twenty hits. It was 11.40 p.m. Incredibly, within twenty minutes they had their twenty Facebook hits! Skate for Macca Day was off and rolling.

With some help from youth worker Gary Webb, they enlisted support from police who supplied the barbecue and even the "doof doof" music. It was a particularly poignant moment for many local young people, and the police, because five youths had just died in a tragic car accident not far from one of the skating facilities at Mill Park, to the south of Whittlesea.

Two hundred people turned up to the event and Webb gave out a Macca Award to the best skater. Police and teenagers mingled seamlessly. Shane Warne also made an appearance, and in typical Warnie fashion chatted to the goggle-eyed kids and parents, signed autographs and didn't leave until the event was over.

A week later Ross and Bec were preparing to mark the first anniversary of Black Saturday at Kinglake football ground. Much thought and discussion went into planning the day. Organisers decided to hold two events: one would be private and for the mourners, while the second would be open to the media.

Murrindindi Shire took charge of the proceedings, although some locals were concerned that the shire officers were too far removed from what had transpired at Kinglake on February 7. Their concerns were assuaged when Bec and others who had been directly affected joined the organising committee.

***

So, it was twelve months later. To Ross, each month seemed like it was loaded with a year's worth of agonising pain and personal mayhem. Channel Seven's Nick McCallum interviewed the Buchanans again and the story went to air on *Seven News*, just before the sport. That's where they normally run the colour stories.

During that interview session Wally Spezza said Ross Buchanan was an "inspiration" with amazing "guts and determination". Nick then asked Ross what he thought of his good mate; Ross said Wally was a "bullshit artist". Not surprisingly, those quotes finished up on the editor's floor.

On the morning of the anniversary there was a sad and sombre mood in the Buchanan household. The bereaved were to be given a chance to say a few words at the footy ground ceremony later in the day but Ross's mind was speeding in different directions. He didn't know the right words to use so he went next door to Wally's house for some private thinking time.

Eventually he decided he'd let his music do the talking and he chose one of Neeve's favourite songs. He sat alone in Wally's house rehearsing the tune but he couldn't complete it without breaking down in tears. Ross decided he needed some self-medication and despite promising Bec way back in September he'd give up hard liquor, he unscrewed a bottle of Johnnie Walker whisky which Calum had given him.

By the time Wally rang to find out if everything was OK Ross was flying and he told his mate that he was fine; he was just trashing his neighbour's house.

At the footy oval the tears flowed uncontrollably. When it was Ross's turn up on stage he took three chairs with him and explained to the crowd that one was for Macca, who would normally play drums, one was for little Neeve who would normally help on vocals and the third chair was for Uncle Dan who would do the videoing. Three chairs that twelve months previously would have been occupied now stood starkly empty on stage.

Ross sang a verse for each of them then asked everyone to join in the fourth verse, which they were to sing on behalf of all the loved ones who'd perished. After that the tempo of the day lifted with music that was more upbeat and, somewhat bizarrely, clowns even made an appearance. It was as if people were unsure of what was the appropriate tone for the first anniversary of Black Saturday.

Days later a grief and bereavement counsellor rang Ross to congratulate him on his performance on stage. He of course didn't see it as a "performance" for the crowd, it was simply a very personal tribute to loved ones who had been gone a year. Ross waited a few days then phoned her back at 1 A.M. to set her straight.

CHAPTER 4

ROSS AND BEC SAY "THANK YOU"

More local artists told Ross they wanted to be part of the Thank You Melbourne concert; however, the organising crew still didn't have the money to pay for a venue, nor did they even have a confirmed date. Time was running out.

The Myer Music Bowl was available on March 7, a day that was closing in fast but it was a venue with a rental price beyond their means. Melbourne's Federation Square was available a month later, on April 7, and that was starting to look like a winner even though it was a midweek day when people would have less free time to attend.

Bec, Mahony, Wally, Ross and others met with government and VBRRA officials as well as Blue Ribbon people and many more potential helpers. They stayed up until the early hours of the morning sending out emails asking for help, but they still couldn't secure enough dollars and they remained uncertain about the $35,000 promised by the premier.

Then came a blow of such force it rendered the normally gregarious Ross Buchanan momentarily speechless.

They saw advertisements for *another* "Thank You Melbourne" concert.

Australian rock icon John Farnham was to perform at the Myer Music Bowl on March 6 with tickets around $90 each and all proceeds to go to the Alfred Hospital. It was to be Melbourne's chance to thank the firefighters who had battled bravely and indefatigably on February 7.

Ross and his crew were aghast. Their free concert, featuring mostly local artists, was about to be drowned out by The Voice, as Farnham is known, and they were faced with the prospect of abandoning weeks of work. They manned the phones and the emails and contacted every potential ally they could find in their fight to stop the Farnham concert.

Wally and Mahony were particularly angry and refused to even consider walking away from their venture. They demanded a meeting with the Farnham concert organisers. At that meeting the Kinglakers made it clear the town wasn't big enough for both concerts, certainly not so close together. They pointed out that the Kinglake people really did deserve priority. Farnham's backers graciously deferred to Wally and Mahony; their concert wouldn't go ahead.

Ross heard later that almost $100,000 had been spent on promoting and marketing the Farnham Myer Music Bowl concert; that figure was never verified.

Coincidently, gale force winds, severe thunderstorms, flash flooding and hail stones as big as golf balls hit Melbourne on March 6. Thousands of cars were damaged in the massive storms and trees fell on houses. Ross, Bec and Aiden had to stop in their car on top of Melbourne's Bolte Bridge as one of the storms ripped across the city. For fifteen minutes the hail and winds lashed their vehicle, and so severe was the storm they thought their safety was at risk. They also couldn't help thinking what would've happened if the John Farnham concert had gone ahead on that day in the open air at the Myer Music Bowl.

❧

Eventually the $35,000 in state government backing came through, although no one seemed clear as to precisely which department was coughing up the money. Corporates also chipped in a few thousand dollars and Ross, reluctantly, called on Promains and Orange Pumps again.

More money came from the Reece company in Whittlesea and even the Melbourne Lord Mayor's office, while local MP Danielle Green allowed them to work out of her office to save on phone costs and photocopying.

Christine Nixon's PA, Jennifer Howard, also came on board and slowly things began to fall into place. Local wood turner Glen Barlow, who had been trapped near the Naylors' house during the fires, and blacksmith Ray Brasser agreed to create a sculpture for the occasion.

Children from schools in fire-ravaged Strathewen, Marysville and Kinglake were to sing at the concert.

Ross and Wally had undergone some media training in 2009 so when the TV crews agreed to speak to the kids about the concert and instead changed the subject to a recent theft at Strathewen School, they were quickly put back on course by the Kinglake boys.

In the week leading up to the concert, the pace of the preparation began to change. For every step forward, they were now taking just half a step backwards. They were also handling a lot of their own promotional work after some problems with the promotions company that was originally engaged to help them. Channel 10's weatherman Mike Larkin agreed to do the MC work at the concert and to also feature them during his news segment.

Channel Seven's *Sunrise* program also said it might do something with the Kinglake people, but high-profile comedian Ross Noble told them he'd be a "no show". Noble, one of Britain's leading stand-up exponents, pulled out of the concert because he had to rush home to be with his ill father. This was a significant blow to the Kinglakers because Noble had shared their suffering through the bushfires and their aftermath. He and his Australian wife had been living at St Andrews on a farm which was destroyed on Black Saturday. They lost all their possessions. They returned permanently to the UK.

But still, on the eve of the concert, the positives far outweighed the problems. They were to perform at Melbourne's Federation Square in a concert that was all their own work. They were as nervous as they were excited.

※

On the big day Bec and Mahony focused their finely tuned organisational skills on the concert, which had blown out to ten hours of music leavened with some poetry and personal accounts of Black Saturday. They were understaffed and over worked, their assistants were mostly amateurs with no major event experience, and they were working at a site they had little technical knowledge of.

Somehow they managed to pull it off. The music reached out to passers-by and many who came to listen were also drawn to the bushfire artwork, much of it by local children, which bordered the stage area.

Federation Square officials said 32,000 people saw the concert. It made news around Australia and, Ross was told, in some places internationally. It all ran like clockwork thanks to the two women pulling the levers. It was a triumphal moment for the people from many of the bushfire regions.

Ross (in white T shirt) and the Pay Dirt band performing at Federation Square in Melbourne. Names of bushfire affected towns are written on the stage banner. (Pic: family collection.)

Premier Brumby appeared on stage and was presented with the Brasser-Barlow sculpture, which thereafter was dubbed "Mr Gumby". Mr Gumby now resides in Museum Victoria.

To the onlookers it seemed Ross Buchanan was in his own world. In fact, many who have watched him perform on stage believe it's one of the few places he's at peace. However, he refused to sing the "Kinglake Song" which was a repertoire staple that had been such a big hit in April the previous year at Kinglake's Rising from the Ashes day.

On that occasion thousands, including John Brumby, Bill Shorten and Peter Garrett, had joined in the chorus "Kinglake is where I want to be". It had been a reaffirmation of their way of life, just weeks after the fires.

Now so much had happened and so much had changed. Kinglake was, from Ross Buchanan's perspective, just a place to survive in.

∾

Media interest in the Federation Square concert was more intense than Ross had expected. There were abundant TV cameras and reporters. In fact, the media was so thick on the ground that Ross was wary. He suspected they weren't there just for a good news story and that they were really hunting for Christine Nixon, who was fighting to keep her career alive after some embarrassing revelations.

The *Herald Sun* newspaper had disclosed Nixon's movements after the then police chief commissioner left the Incident Control Centre in Melbourne late in the afternoon on Black Saturday. The Bushfires Royal Commission had been told that while visiting the ICC the police chief was satisfied that everything that could be done was being done as disaster loomed. Despite being informed it was likely some people would die in the bushfires, Nixon had still departed the emergency room. She told the Royal Commission she had absolute confidence in her senior officers and she intended to monitor developments from home. However, the *Herald Sun* learned that Nixon actually went out to a hotel for dinner with two friends. Worse still, she hadn't made any calls from the hotel seeking fire emergency updates, nor had she received any updates.

There was public disbelief and then dismay. State opposition leader Ted Baillieu said Nixon had to resign as VBRRA boss. The media was hot on her trail and were hoping she would surface at the Thank You Melbourne concert; ideally she'd appear in time for them to file stories for evening news bulletins.

However, many people, and Bec in particular, were protective of a woman who'd built personal bridges into the fire-impacted communities. Christine Nixon was, importantly, very approachable and accommodating. She had their support. They also believed that the Black Saturday fires were so ferocious that it was beyond the capacity of Nixon, or any other individual, to alter the devastating outcome. This view of course is not completely consistent with evidence tendered to the Bushfires Royal Commission. As we have seen, the Kinglake ridge people have a right to feel that they were let down by authorities in terms of CFA fire warnings and information dissemination.

But there was also one other reason Christine Nixon had their backing. Many thought that it was best to leave her in charge of distributing the hundreds of millions of dollars of donated money rather than seeing her forced out of a job that was only half completed. They believed Nixon was best placed to account for all the money that had already been spent.

When the media repeatedly quizzed the Kinglakers at the concert about Nixon's Black Saturday failings they replied that they wanted her to stay on with VBRRA. The media sensed that Christine Nixon's head was about to roll, it was a significant story that would cast the Brumby State Government in a bad light for appointing her in the first place. But the Kinglakers weren't about to help the reporters carry her to the chopping block.

As the TV news deadlines passed, the crews began to leave, and when Nixon eventually did emerge from her self-imposed solitude there was only one camera still rolling.

The band Ruckus played the final song of the night, "I Am Australian", and then Bec strode out on stage and made a rare public appearance. She was there to introduce a "very special guest, Christine Nixon". The crowd gave the besieged woman a rousing cheer and she in turn thanked them for their backing. Her immediate fate was probably decided that night; if the bushfire survivors had turned on her publicly then Premier Brumby would have had little option but to cut her loose. But it was as if Nixon had been adopted by people from the fire regions as one of their own. They favoured her over the media, which were often viewed as cynical and self-serving.

The sole TV camera, belonging to Channel Nine, kept filming, although some crowd members pushed and harassed the cameraman.

One man pushed so hard he slipped and fell to the ground, latching on to the cameraman's pants on the way down.

So Channel Nine had its footage of Nixon fronting the bushfire crowd. Ross and the others then agreed to give the networks some of their own video that had been shot at the event. This included footage of Bec and Nixon on stage. Bec was horrified; she had painstakingly kept a low media profile since February 2009 but now she would be all over the TV news.

She was angry with Ross yet again, or more correctly, she was still angry with him. Despite the euphoria which followed the concert on the Wednesday night they had parted on hostile terms. Ross had felt like a beer or three to celebrate the triumph of their months of hard work, Bec had lost interest in him when he began drinking and she headed home to Kinglake, leaving Ross in the city.

Ross began thinking that the night would have been perfect if Macca, Neeve and Dan had been there.

The following day Bec and Ross made their peace, again. Calum had already left for Europe. He'd concluded that all the counsellors in the world couldn't change the one thing in his life he wanted to alter. He wanted his brother and sister back.

Calum could see no value in talking to the media either. In the overall context of the personal losses the Buchanans had suffered, Calum thought the media were irrelevant. Or worse, the media were often an unrelenting predator akin to foxes returning nightly to the same farmyard where they'd once found a meal.

Bec had many reasons to get on a plane and follow him. She was involved in the memorial research, she needed to escape the omnipresent whiff of tragedy at Kinglake and, most importantly, she wanted to meet her son overseas. Christine Nixon reached into her own pocket to help pay for the trip.

Bec and Aiden left Melbourne and visited memorials in the United Kingdom, France, Italy, New Zealand and North America, and she later prepared a report for Murrindindi Shire Council.

It was clear that a substantial memorial to the Black Saturday victims would require a central feature along with a sheltered area for visitors. The construction bill, not to mention a maintenance bill, was likely to cost far in excess of the $600,000 which had been set aside for the Victorian project. But something unrelated to the memorial tour caught Bec by surprise and gave her reason to consider her future. She fell in love with the township of Whistler in Canada and decided she wanted to live there.

Reconciling the attraction of a fresh start in a resort wonderland with the pull of her immediate family in Kinglake is something she would have to work through.

❧

Barely three months after the Thank You Melbourne concert, Christine Nixon stood down as VBRRA chairwoman. During that time she had been called back before the Bushfires Royal Commission.

Nixon maintained her defence that there was nothing more she could have done to help on Black Saturday and was confident the Incident Control Centre was in the hands of experienced and qualified officers. However, in hindsight, she regretted the decision to leave the ICC and have dinner.

Counsel assisting the Royal Commission, Jack Rush, said Nixon had "attempted to deceive" while giving her original evidence and was guilty of a "deliberate omission". That is, the fact that she went out to a pub for dinner with friends.

She resigned just as the federal election was called and said the timing was purely coincidental and not designed to consign her decision to the inner pages of the newspapers because the political headlines grabbed the front page. Nixon said she had decided the appropriate time to resign was at a meeting of the bushfire region community recovery committees and that date had been set for some weeks.

She had been earning more than $340,000 per annum as VBRRA boss. After quitting Nixon offered to continue helping the victims at no cost.

Just ten days following her resignation the Royal Commission released its final report. It found she had erred by leaving the ICC at a time of crisis and she, and others, failed to demonstrate effective leadership.

Crucially, the report didn't conclude that the former police chief had deliberately misled the Royal Commission.

After the Thank You Melbourne concert Ross had two days to complete his own submission for the Bushfires Royal Commission.

He was concerned about just how comprehensive the hearings had been. Why wasn't Cameron Caine called? Why didn't the Commission want to hear from Lynn Gunter, the popular mayor of Murrindindi Shire, which included not only the devastated Kinglake ridge and Flowerdale areas but also the obliterated township of Marysville?

Gunter was given a rousing reception at the Thank You Melbourne concert and was widely respected and liked by many in the shire. She eventually stood down as mayor when she opposed moves to increase rates to help finance bushfire recovery.

Ross believed others should also have had their say before the commissioners.

As part of his own submission he included the controversial letter he sent to Kevin Rudd, Christine Nixon and others midway through 2009 complaining that bereaving families had been left high and dry financially. He also asked for his submission to receive "full exclusion" from the public record. In other words, he didn't want the media to be able to report on what he said to the Commission.

Ross had read many of the submissions and been concerned at the level of detail that had been made public about some of the Black Saturday deaths. He felt it was almost becoming voyeuristic and he didn't want the media revisiting the horrific events at Number One Reserve Road.

Cam and another friend went with Ross when he met Commission officials to discuss his submission and subsequent appearance. When the time came to ask for "full exclusion" the official replied he wasn't the person who could enforce that rule. Fearing that he could be left at the media's mercy Ross exploded. He yelled, "Get me the fucking person who can then!"

That night Ross received a phone call from the Royal Commission. He had been granted full exclusion, which meant no one would be able to read his submission for 99 years.

When it came time to front the hearings Ross told the commissioners he had heartfelt sympathy for them because of the traumatic evidence they had been forced to sit through. He said they must be very strong people to listen to the harrowing details of so many deaths and he hoped they had friends and family to confide in during the difficult moments they must surely endure.

A number of friends were with him as once more he ventured down the nightmarish path of the events of February 7. Wally and Cam were among them, Jan Chambers was there too. Since losing her daughters Mel and Pen in the tragedy Jan had gone through a particularly tough time and locals had started a campaign to try and find her somewhere to live.

Ross was also granted permission to re-work the original statement he gave to police after the fires because there were some aspects of it he was uncomfortable with. In particular he was concerned about an assertion that there were 50 acres of cleared land next door to the Buchanan house in National Park Road. This implies that his home was safer than it actually was and it's then only a brief leap of logic to ask why he would take his children elsewhere if his home provided reasonable refuge.

After the hearings he and the friends retired to the pub.

⁂

Ross left to join Bec and Aiden overseas three days after appearing at the Royal Commission in mid-May 2010. Bec's memorial quest was in full swing. She had vowed to herself not to let anything prevent her from contributing to a poignant and appropriate memorial for the hometown where her children had grown up. The hometown where two of them had died, along with her brother, many friends and others she had met through the Buchanan pump business.

So many memories and emotions were locked away in her heart. She recalled vividly how a business cheque had arrived in the mailbox the week after Black Saturday. It was from the McIvor family in Strathewen. The entire family had been wiped out in the fires. The cheque was never cashed.

Bec was on a mission to honour all these people and she had to get it right.

Looking back she later realised that leaving Australia, with a purpose in mind, helped her avoid some severe mental health issues. She had no doubt she was heading for a padded cell.

Similarly, the overseas venture played a key role in simply helping Aiden and Calum cope with their own grief. It also opened Aiden's eyes to what a truly remarkable place our world is.

As Prince William had promised when she met him at Whittlesea, he did everything he could to assist her trip. He organised for his staff to show Bec and Aiden through St James's Palace in Pall Mall. This stunning structure was built by Henry VIII in the 1530s and is King Charles III's official residence. What the Buchanans' didn't foresee was that a uniform was waiting for Aiden to wear and he, and Bec, were accompanied through the palace by royal attendees. What they also didn't foresee was the compassionate gesture that awaited them in Queen's Chapel.

Inside the chapel were three candles. They had been lit to honour the memory of Neeve, Macca and Danny.

The whole experience was overwhelming and it put Bec in a very good place emotionally to meet up with Ross who was flying in from Melbourne. Unfortunately, the family reunion was delayed because Ross had a run-in with officialdom. He was waylaid by customs at Heathrow Airport because he couldn't tell them where he would be staying in London. Bec hadn't sent him those details. After some frantic phone calls he was waved through. Ross had arrived in time to join Bec and Aiden on their trip to the National Memorial Arboretum in Staffordshire. Prince William is the arboretum's patron.

Set on 150 acres at the western end of Britain's National Forest, the arboretum is home to 300 memorials. William had organised for the Buchanans to be given a fully escorted tour of the sprawling facility. Three hundred memorials represents a considerable number of concepts and designs to absorb during a one-day visit. However, one memorial in particular left an indelible imprint on Bec. It was the SIDS memorial and it takes the form of a hidden garden that provides a place of tranquillity and reflection. Replete with beautiful gardens and bordered by hedges there is ample seating to accommodate those seeking a private moment to remember their deceased children.

Thousands of rocks are scattered through the memorial. On each rock is the name of the child who died and the date of the tragedy. Those details have been recorded in permanent marker by the bereaving mothers.

Bec fought back the tears at the SIDS memorial but it also reminded her that she was a part of a very broad church, the church of grieving mothers. In this church she would never be alone.

The Staffordshire visit also revealed that some memorials, although built with the best intentions, were ill conceived. They were in urgent need of repair despite being constructed in recent years. The message was clear: choose materials that were enduring and a concept that required the least maintenance.

William had also arranged for the Buchanans to meet with the London bombing 7/7 memorial architect and consulting group, and for them to visit the Hyde Park water memorial to his own mother Diana, Princess of Wales.

The Buchanans then rendezvoused with Calum in Scotland before going their separate ways. Ross headed home while Bec and Aiden went on to visit other sites in the United Kingdom and the USA.

Of all the memorials they visited, two of them, in Bec's view, were particularly poignant and could provide useful tips for the designers of the Kinglake monument – the SIDS garden and the white granite memorial in Wales to the victims of the Aberfan tragedy. One hundred and forty-four people, including 116 children, were buried in 1966 when coal waste engulfed a village in South Wales. The memorial of white stone arches makes a simple but enduring statement.

Ross arrived home at the end of June. He was too jetlagged and depressed to alter his original police statement. His depression stemmed from a perception that there was more darkness and despondency at Kinglake than at any time since the fires. Perhaps that perception was also coloured around the edges by something as prosaic as an overseas venture coming to an end.

By the time his mental disposition had improved and he was ready to re-work his statement, the Commission told him it was too late. So the document was never altered. When the report came out in August Ross was more convinced than ever that some people who should have given evidence weren't called upon. People who had firsthand knowledge of what worked and what failed during the initial recovery period were also overlooked by the Royal Commission.

Cam Caine and Roger Wood in particular should have been called, in Ross's view. They were at the heart of the disaster and as Ross pointed out, "I thought our police-emergency service's communication and coordination needed to be dissected so Cam and Roger would have been of great benefit for the future."

However, it's clear from the Commission's terms of reference that the focus was on "causal issues" rather than recovery. Not surprisingly, Ross wrote a pithy email about the perceived failings of the Royal Commission.

Beccy Cole

Before heading overseas in 2010 Bec had bonded with leading musician Beccy Cole at the Whittlesea Country Music Festival. Only twelve months earlier she had watched in horror from that same festival as the bushfire raced up the mountain towards Kinglake West.

Cole is an award-winning performer with eight albums to her credit, including three which charted in the top 40.

It was their 2010 meeting that inspired Cole to write the song "Australian Woman", which was nominated for a Golden Guitar award in 2011 and 2012 at Tamworth, Australia's famous country music festival.

When the two women first met, Cole noticed the tattoos on Bec's arm; they honour her children and Danny. She became aware of the wrenching events Bec had been through and remarked that Bec was "the strongest woman she knew". Bec replied, "How would you know?" to which Cole responded, "Because you are still here."

Cole needed help to finish writing the song because it's so emotionally over-powering, and she seldom performs it for that same reason.

When Bec arrived home from her overseas trip she saw Cole performing in Albury and heard "Australian Woman" for the first time. Cole told her she was particularly nervous about singing "Australian Woman" because she wasn't certain she could complete the song without crying.

By the end of the song it was Rebecca Buchanan who was in tears.

CHAPTER 5

THE CAMPAIGN TRAIL

CHRISTINE NIXON'S RESIGNATION had indeed been pushed off the front pages by the announcement of the federal election, which was called by Prime Minister Julia Gillard on 17 July 2010. There was to be a frenetic five-week campaign.

Gillard had rolled Kevin Rudd in a stunning late-night leadership coup in late June when Labor's factional heavyweights lost patience with him. With Rudd as leader the government's primary vote had fallen to the mid-30s, that is, only just over one third of voters would give the current government a "tick" as first preference at an election. Rudd's popularity was in a nosedive.

The factional leaders had begun to sense electoral defeat. Rudd was being pummelled over a number of issues including climate change, a botched home insulation scheme, a possibly wasteful education building program that was introduced to help stave off recession, and more lately, a new mining tax.

The electorate was initially smitten with Julia, Australia's first woman prime minister, and she played especially well in her home state of Victoria where Tony Abbott's conservative family values and "pugnacious Sydney attitudes" were a turn off.

Labor candidate Rob Mitchell was eager to capitalise on the change and pointed out repeatedly in the weeks ahead that a vote for him was a vote for Julia Gillard, while a vote for Cameron Caine was a vote for Tony Abbott. Abbott was the former champion of the detested WorkChoices industrial relations scheme and an arch conservative to boot.

From Cameron's perspective it probably meant he'd have to find another couple of percentage points somewhere. Fortunately, the weeks leading up to July 17 had presented him with a one-off chance to hog the media spotlight.

After Prime Minister Gillard set the election date the media were legally obliged to give equal coverage to both major candidates, but in the weeks prior Cam was free to soak up as much of the limelight as he could attract. He had a small win on this front, although there were two serious impediments to a Cam Caine media assault.

Firstly, he was still in police uniform and consequently his public comments were censored by his employer. For example, Cameron felt very strongly that bushfire recovery was lagging but to be critical of that situation was to also criticise his employer, the state government. Nevertheless, media releases were put out in his name until, just prior to the election being announced, he was given a warning by his superiors.

The second issue came from another set of superiors. Liberal bosses were wary their political neophyte would make comments damaging his own credibility, or worse, the good name of his party. They fended off media requests from Channel Seven, Sky News, ABC TV and others believing Cam wasn't ready to be interviewed just yet. 104 (Liberal headquarters) needed Cam to master as many of the party policies as possible before he was let loose. He was given the policy bible, a folder amounting to around 100 pages which he had to study and digest over the week or two prior to the official commencement of the campaign. Mastering the detail contained in that manual was never going to happen.

The breadth of the topics it covered was staggering and getting his head around the various policies was a daily challenge, especially when new policies were being announced and others were being refined.

Of course, those policy details also hid some pesky little "detail devils" that only appeared once you drilled down further into them. For example, Tony Abbott and the Liberals assessed that there was genuine unease in the community about the arrival of asylum seeker boats off Australia's north-west coast. Part of the strategy for combating the arrivals was to simply turn the boats around. The slogan had a convincingly simplistic ring to it but lurking just below the surface was the problematic issue of the international legalities, let alone the practicalities, of turning boats around on the high seas.

Any journalist looking for a quick and easy mark in the lead up to the campaign could succinctly have led Cam down the asylum seeker path and then mugged the would-be member for McEwen with some tricky but not unreasonable questions.

After a fortnight of interview rejections, 104 realised that Cam had to be let off the leash at some stage and they decided he should honour a Channel Seven request. Cam would talk to Nick McCallum.

"Piss off, mate." That was the no frills response from a man Cam approached with a political brochure in the Wallan shopping centre. Cam had gone there to shoot some footage with McCallum.

Cam's story was a compelling yarn beginning with the fires, then the recovery and now the shot at federal parliament. But it wasn't compelling enough to deter some voters from suggesting he piss off.

It was also a harbinger of the tough campaign road ahead.

Cam and the Channel Seven reporter also talked with the Butterworths about the spiralling costs of rebuilding after the fires; they then travelled fifty kilometres away to Gisborne to meet a local group campaigning for a new indoor sports stadium.

"Cam's story" was a good solid yarn about a local hero looking to head off in a new direction in life and crash through some daunting barriers. Whether it would help convince people to vote for a former copper was another issue entirely. The senior constable was allowed to stay in the police force while he campaigned, until the election was formally called at which point he had to resign.

Cam had taken Nick McCallum to Wallan because the Liberal

strategy had been to open a campaign office in the shopping centre there. Wallan is close to the new population growth corridor north of Melbourne. However, it was also about eighty kilometres from Fran Bailey's office in Healesville, which reflects just how big the electorate of McEwen is. In fact, it's roughly the size of Belgium.

Some nights Cam would drive for over an hour to a meeting and discover just three people had turned up. His car became his new workplace, after he'd finished his police shift.

In terms of time commitment it was a tough gig. It was also expensive because his police income had dried up at the same time he was forced to shell out for extra expenses, such as paying for all his electorate travel. Fortunately, 104 eventually kicked in with some financial help.

He also had some other issues to sort through.

Fran Bailey had made it abundantly clear from their first meeting that Cam had more to learn from her than vice versa. She was a wizened political warrior who'd spent nearly two decades in the saddle. Bailey had fought long and hard to control her own destiny. She was a formidable mentor. Campaign manager Mark Beacham and 104 were also in Cam's corner. But on any given issue Bailey didn't necessarily see eye-to-eye with Beacham or 104. That mix would sometimes change and there were occasions Beacham and Bailey didn't agree with directions from 104, or Beacham didn't agree with either of the others.

Then once the campaign was underway, yet another ingredient was added to the sometimes volatile cocktail: 104 asked Liberal Senator Scott Ryan to work with Cameron. Ryan towed the party line and thus could be at odds with Bailey and/or Beacham.

The local Liberal candidate in the Victorian state election, Mike Laker, was also eager to help Cam and offer advice. He was generous with his time, offering to catch trains into the city any morning to hand out "how to vote" cards and to also attend any functions where Cam might need some backup.

Laker had mastered the art of "pollie speak". With great verbal dexterity he could deflect a probing question from an interlocutor and wax lyrically about the issue at hand without actually making a commitment to policy change. It's an art form practiced and perfected by politicians who learn to avoid giving a direct answer.

Cam had been giving and expecting direct answers all his working life so he put that pollie speak method in the too hard drawer, alongside the policy bible. It also occurred to him that Mike Laker was a very capable politician with slick presentation skills and a wide grasp of policy issues. He concluded Mike would make a good federal member!

Ironically, Cam thought he was more suited to state politics with its focus on everyday meat and potato issues such as crime, transport, education and health. In contrast, federal politics seemed remote and esoteric.

Cam also recruited a helper in the Wallan office when Carmel, a Liberal Party member from the west of the electorate, volunteered her time. She was to prove a godsend later when hundreds of people began calling the office wanting advice on voting practices and policy issues, or simply to abuse the candidate.

One of the first visitors to the new office was an elderly local man wearing a wide brimmed hat and boasting only a few teeth in the upper and lower gums. He had a special request for the would-be member for McEwen. He demanded Cam do something about the number of advertisements on commercial TV. He was particularly aggrieved that his favourite show, *Heartbeat*, was being "ruined by the ads".

Another visitor had more serious issues to raise.

Just six days after Prime Minister Gillard announced the August 21 election, a woman called Natalie broke down in tears in the office. She was so distressed that Carmel phoned Cameron for help and he drove across to Wallan.

Natalie was from Clonbinane, not far from where the Kilmore East blaze began on Black Saturday. She believed her small community had been overlooked by those administering the bushfire recovery. She said she couldn't sleep at night because of the red tape tying up the rebuilding of her house, and she was also desperate to find additional counselling for her son. Natalie said her situation was hopeless and she was desperate.

It was a similar refrain to what he was hearing at Kinglake and elsewhere, but Natalie really struck a chord when she told Cam that if fire ever threatened them again her family would rather perish fighting the flames than go through the hell they were currently living in.

Cam was shaken. He vowed there and then to push harder on behalf of the bushfire victims. That weekend he met Wally and Ross at a big Kinglake Football Netball Club function. They had already arranged to speak to Nick McCallum on the following Wednesday about the failings of the recovery and agreed to bring the Clonbinane people on board as well.

Cam also decided to hold an open meeting late on the Wednesday afternoon for locals who felt they were being left behind by the bushfire recovery. Prior to doing the Channel Seven McCallum interview the Clonbinane people met with Ross, Wally, Cam, Lynn Gunter and some other Kinglakers at a local bakery. They found they had a remarkable amount in common. People nodded sagely as one after the other talked about their frustration with bureaucrats as they tried to rebuild, insurance companies that weren't "playing ball" and their fears that they would be cut adrift when the counsellors were withdrawn.

In many cases anger had overtaken their frustration. However, it was a cathartic moment for people from different bushfire-ravaged communities to get together and exchange stories.

A couple of hours after that meeting about thirty locals, and some media, sat inside the Kinglake clubrooms going over similar territory. It was a tense atmosphere. Some made it clear they had had a gutful of government authorities and were ready to confront them. For these people there was nowhere else to turn except to confrontation.

In particular they needed help and advice as they picked their way through a minefield of rebuilding regulations. Cam was confronted by a range of different problems, but what was he to do about them?

In contrast, Rob Mitchell, who was locked in to supporting the state Labor Government, had been publicly claiming that people recovering from the bushfires were "moving ahead at their own pace". It was a position that was galling to many.

There were also growing fears that after the state election (which was due in November after the federal poll, and after VBRRA closed its doors) whatever problems people had would receive less attention.

It was suggested that the Victorian Government should be asked to include bushfire recovery in a single ministerial portfolio so that when VBRRA wound down there would be one desk where the buck could stop.

This was considered to be a not unreasonable request given the scale of the Black Saturday disaster. It also gave Cam something tangible to take away from the meeting, something he could push for publicly that would be of long-term benefit to the people of Kinglake, Marysville, Clonbinane and the other bushfire communities.

A media release was to be issued with Cam calling on the state government to make bushfire recovery and reconstruction the responsibility of one minister as soon as VBRRA ceased functioning. That seemed the least he could do for the people who had poured their hearts out to him, and to each other, over the preceding four hours.

It also meant Cameron could further enhance his reputation as a spokesman for people in the bushfire areas so if the media needed someone to talk with who was in touch with local sentiment, and not beholden to a government department, they could come to him.

But Cam hadn't counted on the complexities of the federal–state system getting in the way. No sooner had the proposed "one minister" idea been put forward than word came back down the line that it was a non-starter.

As Senator Scott Ryan explained it, this was a state issue and federal politicians, or even likeable potential federal MPs such as Cam, couldn't go stomping through someone else's patch. The idea was never broached again.

Bushfire recovery is a complex matter and there's no single solution to the many complaints, but the "one minister" angle gave the story some strong focus and the proposal would also have given hope to many that their concerns, and angst, would end up being appraised in one office with a focus on one issue.

The decision not to run with the idea also potentially robbed Cam of some metropolitan media coverage and, more importantly, made him look impotent in the eyes of the local constituents who had attended the Kinglake meeting.

There were further state versus federal complications three days later when the much-awaited Bushfires Royal Commission report was released. Again the Feds were to defer to the state, with Victorian opposition leader Ted Baillieu (Liberal) making most of the running on the issue.

A shadow minister, Andrew Robb, was the ranking Federal Liberal in Victoria and was given the green light to make a statement.

Cam wasn't restricted in his comments; it was simply a case of not being high enough in the pecking order to be put in front of the TV cameras. So any potential advantages in having a Kinglake hero and marginal seat candidate address the issue were lost. The spotlight wasn't big enough for all of them.

Baillieu committed a state Liberal Government to acting on all sixty-seven recommendations handed down by the Royal Commission, a stance that was strongly supported by Fran Bailey. However, one of those recommendations was for the government to buy back properties in high-risk bushfire areas. But Cam was concerned that if a homeowner with a property adjacent to a forest was asked to sell up, then that property would eventually be returned to its natural state and the next house in the street would then be exposed. The policy could have a domino effect on rural communities and could potentially turn some smaller villages into ghost towns.

The Caines also had firsthand experience of the vagaries of bushfires. Even though they lived alongside a heavily timbered creek, which supported a dense understorey, their house had survived the bushfires almost unscathed. Yet it was possible their block of land could be described as "high risk". Cameron strongly believed that if people chose to live next to forests they had to accept the bushfire risk and be well drilled on precautions to take in times of bushfire danger.

His public championing of this issue would have undermined the Baillieu message and if asked for comment by the media he would have been candid and honest, even if it meant upsetting the Liberal bosses. But no interview requests came in, with one exception.

In the week prior to the release of the Royal Commission report in July a number of media organisations had asked to speak to Cam; ABC TV's breakfast program suggested perhaps they wait until *after* everyone had read the report.

The show was co-hosted by Virginia Trioli, a journalist with a fearsome reputation for roughing up politicians and a shark-nosed ability to detect blood when guests were ill-prepared for her line of questioning.

The ABC, like many other outlets, was doing a general piece on the crucial seat of McEwen and wanted to speak to Cam and Rob Mitchell. The producers understood that the contents of the Royal Commission obviously meant a great deal to the people of the electorate. The segment presented Cameron with an ideal opportunity to grab the high ground from Mitchell on what would surely be the story of the day.

However, on the Monday morning following the release of the report there was a thick fog in Kinglake that not only robbed Cameron of an imposing backdrop for his interview but also seemed to harm the reception at the outside broadcast site and made the questions difficult to hear.

Cam had spent the previous day trawling through the report and refining his response to the sixty-seven recommendations but Trioli simply brushed over what had been the biggest story of the weekend and tried to pin Cam on policy issues. He'd devoted hours to preparing for questions that didn't come.

When she asked about "health" Cam was able to point to his support for the medical Super Clinic at Wallan, which was a key plank in Labor's local election campaign and was something the Liberals felt compelled to match.

Trioli arrogantly dismissed it as a "Rudd Government policy" and moved on. What she didn't realise, or chose not to pursue, was the fact that despite condemning the Super Clinics as a waste of money the

Liberals were locked into building thirty-two of them. Shadow Health Minister Peter Dutton had visited Wallan only a couple of weeks earlier and explained to Cam that a Liberal Government would honour contracts that had already been signed, but they certainly didn't want to publicly promote the Super Clinic concept. So the Liberals were committed to spending hundreds of millions of dollars on a policy they didn't believe in. A policy that Cameron was publicly supporting in Wallan.

Trioli could have drawn Cam on this issue, it was messy and it had the potential to blow back on Cam, Dutton and Abbott. Wallan had been signed, but importantly another Super Clinic just over the southern boundary of the electorate in South Morang was part of the second group of contracts and therefore wouldn't go ahead under a Liberal Government. This would have been disadvantageous to people in that area.

Cam correctly told the local media during the Dutton visit, and he also told Trioli, that the money would still be spent on health care at Wallan. From the viewpoint of the local electorate it was a crucially important commitment. But what about South Morang in the new outer suburbs with their thousands of young voters?

Cam continued to hold his ground under some searching Trioli questions but he didn't display a coherent grasp of policy. He looked reasonably comfortable on television even though the calm exterior belied the internal storms that the former local cop grappled with as he tried to fend off one of the ABC's political head bangers.

Doubtlessly the interview produced more negatives than positives.

When Rob Mitchell spoke after Cam he strategically chose Wallan, not far from the Liberal office, as his outside broadcast site. In some balanced interviewing Trioli tackled Mitchell strongly over bushfire recovery, which she knew was Cam's strength. Again Mitchell was unconvincing on this issue but as soon as she moved on to policies he scored heavily.

It was clear that compared to the raw Kinglake copper Rob Mitchell was a convincing and accomplished exponent of pollie speak; it remained to be seen if the electorate would believe him.

A few days later Senator Scott Ryan rang Cam with some encouraging news: a Liberal Government would commit $3.7 million towards a makeover of the sporting complex at Romsey, in the far west of the electorate. It was to be the second biggest local spending announcement in McEwen during the entire campaign.

The project was near the top of the local Macedon Ranges Shire wish list and would provide a huge boost for Romsey, one of the fast-growing communities near the busy Calder Freeway. The announcement would also play to one of Cam's greatest strengths, community sport.

The local media were invited to a press conference at Romsey the following Tuesday, just over a week and a half out from election day.

Cam was in high spirits as he drove to Romsey, about forty minutes from his Kinglake home. The story was sure to get a good run in the local media on the western side of the electorate during the last week of the campaign. But on the trip to Romsey Senator Ryan rang again, this time with an unsettling update. Rob Mitchell's website was boasting about Labor's multi-million-dollar commitment to the Romsey sports complex! Labor had stolen a very timely march on the Liberals.

No sooner had Cam arrived in Romsey than ABC regional radio was on the line wanting to know if a Liberal Government would be prepared to match Labor's big Romsey spend. Cam remained composed and told the ABC that of course he would match it, and he went on to explain how happy he was that the people of Romsey were assured of getting the facilities they deserved no matter who won government.

Ten minutes later he rang the journalist back and added that he was "happy Labor is matching *our* commitment."

Fortunately, Cam still received strong media coverage because he was on site for pictures and interviews. But later in the week even that newspaper publicity was set to come back and bite him.

After the Romsey announcement Cam headed to Wallan but no

sooner had he arrived at the office than his father Jason was on the phone with some disturbing news. All of Cam's campaign posters along busy Plenty Road in the heavily populated southern section of the electorate had been vandalised. It wasn't just a case of someone with a black marker pen defacing the pictures; the posters had been slashed with a sharp implement, perhaps a knife.

At least ten had been destroyed, including one which was high in a tree and another which was in the front yard of a house where a young family lived. Someone had entered that property by clambering over a fence while armed with a knife or other bladed object. The vandalism went well beyond acceptable gamesmanship during an election campaign and was tainted with a vicious element that was a little disturbing, especially for the young family.

Channel Seven's newsroom was contacted and the chief of staff was interested in covering the story. If it was a quiet news day the possibility of a "knifeman in the front yard of a young family's house" had the potential to attract national coverage.

Given Cameron's outstanding background of public service the story was certain to reflect very poorly on the vandals and make it less likely they'd destroy other posters or billboards.

After the call was made to Channel Seven a follow-up call was put through to 104 to let Liberal HQ know the story was in the pipeline. Within twenty minutes 104 called back and canned the story because it would look like Cam was carping or complaining. The message was simple: just get on with the campaign. The Liberals had thrown away a rare opportunity to feature on prime-time TV news.

No one ever accused Rob Mitchell's supporters of slashing the posters, but the following day his own signs had been erected along Plenty Road and Cam's were further destroyed.

༄

Almost as soon as the campaign began, ABC Radio's 774 Melbourne presenter Jon Faine had approached Cameron to appear live on his show, along with the other candidates, a fortnight out from the election. Faine is affable with a good sense of humour but he's a lawyer by profession and is capable of verbally eviscerating any interviewee who is duplicitous or evasive. For politicians it's almost as if there's an enter-at-own risk sign on his studio door.

Every day of the campaign Faine's people had asked Tony Abbott for some of his time and everyday Abbott's people had declined.

Cam, Beacham, Senator Ryan and 104 all thought it was unfair to let Faine loose on the recently retired Kinglake senior constable who was still wading through the cumbersome policy bible.

Fran Bailey was in the other camp; she thought it would be more harmful to allow Mitchell and the Green's Steve Meacher to appear on the program while the Liberal chair sat vacant. Bailey told Cameron he simply had to do it.

Because she was officially retired, with an ill mother in Brisbane, Bailey was well within her rights to just walk away from the campaign and get on with her life. But instead she had chosen to help Cameron when and where she could and her selflessness demanded a certain amount of sacrifice from the new candidate in return.

Cam said he'd do it. He'd go live on air with Faine.

The previous night he, Mitchell and the other candidates had appeared at a public forum in the central Victorian town of Seymour. Cam had performed well, and when he was challenged by a question for which he had no answer he was often able to deliver an anecdote or, failing that, say simply "I don't know."

Cam and Beacham had been concerned Labor would plant stooges in the Seymour forum's audience who would work over the Liberal candidate. But thankfully a great deal of the allotted time was soaked up by people pushing personal barrows, as distinct from policy barrows. One gentleman even insisted on asking the candidates their thoughts about an issue that wasn't on anyone's policy radar, uranium mining.

The audience was respectful of Cam's honest and up-front approach throughout the evening and it was a good tune-up for Faine the following morning.

Cam and Senator Ryan arrived at Bailey's house in Healesville about 7 A.M. for breakfast. They had an hour and a half to prepare and re-visit policies and tactics.

Bailey was keen for Cam not to desert the National Broadband Network (NBN) battlefield and hand Mitchell a clear victory on that issue. Labor promised to pump a staggering $43 billion into wiring almost the entire Australian population into a fibre optic network. It was one of the few big-ticket items in an election campaign being waged under the heavy spending constraints imposed by the global financial crisis.

It was also one of a handful of policy areas where there were significant differences between the two parties and Labor was winning the battle. People were thinking not about the massive jaw-dropping $43 billion investment, but about their access to high-speed downloads and an online future.

In contrast the Liberals were offering a base model Ford at about one seventh the cost of Labor's Rolls Royce. Mark Beacham, an IT specialist, simply shook his head when he saw the Liberal's policy, which sought to cobble together a cable, wireless and satellite network that promised download speeds only one eighth as quick as the NBN.

But Bailey had spotted a network glitch. Labor couldn't afford to run the cable out to communities of under 1,000 people, and that included a large slice of the McEwen population. The people of McEwen needed to be told about the NBN's shortcomings.

She was absolutely certain Faine would want to talk about broadband and was confident Cam had been forewarned and was forearmed.

The 774 outside broadcast was set up in the lounge of the Healesville Hotel, at the foot of the Great Dividing Range and in an area peppered with "green refugees" from the city. There were about sixty people at the tables when Cam and the others arrived. But by the time the candidates went to air, after the nine o'clock news, the room was packed. Faine asked Liberal supporters for a show of hands, two or three people put their arms in the air.

He asked Labor voters to put their hands up, and about one third of the crowd obliged. Faine then sought out Green voters and a forest of hands shot toward the ceiling. Cam's heart sank; he was going to get whacked on climate change, timber felling and other Green issues.

Because he'd been talking with Bailey prior to the nine o'clock news about bushfire issues Faine continued with that theme after introducing the three candidates. This was good, Cam was on home turf. He knew people in the bushfire areas would be listening closely to him and depending on him to speak up on their behalf. Mitchell had said that Black Saturday survivors were recovering at their own pace, a contention Cameron vehemently opposed.

He went on the front foot and sounded assertive and confident. However, Cam was still angry with Mitchell and Meacher over their bushfire question responses and he was keen to continue that debate as Faine moved on to the first policy question.

The topic was parental leave and it should almost have been a free hit for Cam. Perhaps Faine was leading Cameron gently into the debate because the Liberal rookie was up against a Labor pro?

Soon enough the ceiling fell in.

Under the groundbreaking Tony Abbott-inspired Liberal parental leave policy, a mum or dad could take six months leave after the birth of the baby at whatever was the couple's lower wage. So, for example, if the mother earned $1,500 a week she, or her partner, could spend twenty-four weeks at home on that wage plus 9% superannuation. Clearly it was superior to Labor's policy, which was offering just eighteen weeks leave at the minimum wage of $570.

This was Cam's chance to reach out to the families beyond the bushfire regions and score some much-needed points in Melbourne's fringe suburbs where new mums and dads were struggling to pay the house mortgage. But all these facts went out the window because Cam wasn't concentrating; he was still smarting over the bushfire recovery arguments and proceeded to tell Faine about another winning Liberal policy, school rebates.

The Libs were trumping Labor on this issue as well, but it mattered little because it didn't address the question about parental leave.

Faine was quick to lean forward in his chair and challenge Cam. Mitchell also picked up on the major blunder and, from the listener's perspective, seemed to have a better grasp of Liberal policy than the Liberal candidate.

It was a "lost in space" moment. Cam knew and understood the parental leave policy but the combination of the pressure of live radio and the anger he felt over bushfire recovery brought him undone.

Faine moved on to other policies and also took questions from the audience, but the damage had been done.

Towards the end of the debate Faine read out some listener texts. The listener tone wasn't sympathetic to the Liberal candidate, which was not surprising on the ABC where left leaning Labor commentators and talkback callers receive a better reception than on commercial radio outlets. Picking up on the listener feedback, Faine even wondered aloud if Cam was restricting his chances of winning by focusing so strongly on the bushfires.

Cam came back strongly and dominated the last couple of minutes up to the ten o'clock news by pointing out that a great many people in his electorate, who lived in areas like the Macedon Ranges and Warburton, hadn't been touched by the bushfires but over summer often lived with the fire threat.

The election would prove either Faine or Cameron was wrong and in fact it was beginning to look like the latter was the case. Tony Nutt, 104 boss, rang to congratulate Cam for weathering the storm, but also cryptically pointed out that if he lost it wouldn't be his fault. It seemed Victorians, particularly women, were warming to Julia Gillard. Nutt wasn't given to making flippant comments so his conversation could only have been based on some unflattering research. As if to underline that argument the Roy Morgan Research group released a McEwen poll which showed Cam's campaign was pretty much dead in the water.

Men in McEwen were split 50-50 in their voting intentions but among the women Labor was leading by a massive twelve points. More worrying was that the pro-Gillard vote was even stronger in the new housing areas in the electorate's bustling south-west areas.

Cameron wasn't told about the polling but it was clear to many it would take a major change in voting trends for the one-time Kinglake policeman to be elected the following week.

※

If Fran Bailey was upset with Cam's performance on the Faine program she didn't show it. Yes she was concerned that he didn't get the NBN story across and of course she was worried about the parental leave glitch, but her support for the candidate never wavered. She had been working the phones and calling in favours on Cam's behalf. Bailey was candid about her refusal to abide by Liberal Party protocols. If she felt strongly enough about an issue, or a procedural matter, she would simply ignore Liberal Party headquarters.

She did it again when she phoned Tony Abbott's office in a bid to entice the Liberal leader to visit McEwen. Bailey realised that Cam needed all the help he could get to hold on to the seat, and if that meant hosting the leader and his national media entourage, then she would do whatever was necessary to get Abbott to Kinglake.

Bailey had been pushing very hard for a bushfire "early warning detection system", and after more lobbying it was agreed a Liberal Government would contribute $10 million towards its installation. This was a major commitment for the McEwen electorate. The system she favoured could distinguish between smoke and dust or mist over a distance of more than forty kilometres, and it worked 24/7, even scanning the forests while people slept.

The Abbott visit, and the announcement of a bushfire defence system, had the potential to create headlines in the local papers but Bailey was worried that if news of the trip broke early Abbott's people would baulk at attending and the whole media conference would have to be aborted. There had been some incidents during the campaign where people had turned up to heckle Abbott or mock his hairy-chested penchant for wearing brief swimming trunks at the beach.

Bailey was adamant that no local media were to be forewarned about the visit in case the story leaked. So when Abbott duly arrived at Kinglake West CFA on the morning of Saturday August 5 there was a phalanx of photographers, TV cameras and journalists but not one of them was from a local outlet. They filmed and photographed Abbott and Cam inside the CFA building and later tinkling with a fire truck. Alarmingly, but unsurprisingly, the focus of the questions from the national media was on national campaign issues and not bushfire defence. They wanted to know the leader's thoughts on the proposed meeting between Gillard and Rudd later in the day and also on suggestions to re-open Nauru's asylum seeker centre.

Cam and Opposition Leader Tony Abbott campaigning in Kinglake. (Pic: News Limited.)

Cameron barely received any exposure from the visit, although there was a picture and a story buried deep inside the Sunday *Herald Sun* the following day.

A media release for local outlets wasn't cleared by 104 until Monday, two days later. Most local papers insist copy is submitted by Thursday or Friday each week. Because the Abbott visit missed the deadline, and they weren't trusted to sit on the story, the locals didn't publish the bushfire detection announcement until ten or eleven days after the visit.

One editor, Ash Long from the Phoenix, demanded to know why he wasn't given a heads-up about the story and the Abbott visit. Long had been closely covering Kinglake stories since the fires and believed he should have been invited to something as major as the Liberal leader's media conference. When it was explained that the trip had to be kept confidential or Abbott would have pulled the pin, Long slammed the Liberal's media management for being unprofessional.

※

The day after the Healesville "Faine mess" was Friday the 13th and it cast a further pall over the campaign. This was almost a week after the bungled Abbott visit.

At Wallan the campaign office was getting heated calls from people in Hurstbridge who were livid over letters they had received from Cameron alluding to the harsh treatment of a former school principal by the State Education Department. The letter also addressed the contentious sale of the Hurstbridge Secondary College land. These were issues Cameron had only a rudimentary knowledge of and there was no advantage to be gained from buying into the arguments. It was plainly nonsensical for Cam to get involved in red-hot local issues which irritated and split the local community.

A call was put through to the Hurstbridge principal, who did well to contain his anger over the letter, and it was explained that Cameron certainly didn't issue the document and "his people" were eager to find out the source of this dirty tricks campaign.

Coupled with the sign slashing incident from the week before it appeared on the surface as though some of Rob Mitchell's supporters were seeking to undermine and destroy Cameron's election operation.

However, more calls revealed that Cam already knew about the Hurstbridge row, and the letter that sparked it, even though his own office was in the dark. These were local fights that Bailey had been embroiled in and she was keen for 104 to put out the letter in Cam's name. Another call, this one tinged with humiliation, was put through to the Hurstbridge principal explaining that the letter was in fact genuine.

Voters in the seat of McEwen were inundated with publicity from the Liberal and Labor parties during the campaign. In fact, 104 sent out so many letters that a frustrated resident rang the Caines' house after midnight one morning. A bleary-eyed Laura picked up the phone. The man screamed down the line, "Every time I go to the mailbox there's another letter from you people! Stop sending me fucking letters or I'll blow your house up!"

Laura conceded that the man had a valid complaint but it was a disturbing and untimely over reaction. She never discovered who made the call, or how the caller obtained the police officer's phone number.

Another spot fire sprang up further west over that $3.7 million Romsey sports facility commitment. No sooner had one of the local papers published a front-page photo of Cam on Friday 13 than Macedon Ranges Shire councillor Joe Morabito launched an expletive laden tirade down the phone line.

It was just over a week away from the election and Cam desperately needed some things to go right for him.

Morabito wanted to know why two Liberal leaning councillors had been invited to the Romsey media launch, and had their photos in the paper, while he had missed out! He'd been cut out of a huge local story. Morabito said he was the one who'd campaigned long and hard over the last seven years for the sports precinct upgrade and now when it was finally happening he'd been snubbed.

He was assured that the lack of notification was just an oversight rather than a local political conspiracy, but Morabito was having none of it and warned he'd now campaign for Rob Mitchell and that Cam was "fucked in Romsey."

In the meantime, Martin King from MTR (Melbourne Talk Radio) had been doing vox pops in Diamond Creek, in the south of the electorate near Hurstbridge, and wanted to interview the McEwen candidates that same Friday afternoon. Melbourne's newest talk radio station was rating under 2% and was struggling to find listeners, so there was a risk that if Cam agreed to the interview King could go in hard in a bid to give his ratings a shot in the arm.

104 decided there was a huge potential downside to agreeing to the interview but only a small upside, so vetoed it. The knock back prompted King to go on air and demand that Cameron answer the questions that the electorate wanted to hear asked.

One MTR listener rang Bailey and warned that Cam was getting a pasting. She in turn contacted the candidate and told him to forget what 104 was saying, he simply had to respond to the challenge King was throwing at him. Bailey was passionate and insistent.

Cam relented and went live on air after 5 P.M., right in the middle of Drive Time. He was ready to be grilled over parental leave, NBN, health, education and whatever else King would fling at him. Given what had happened the previous day with Faine this interview had the potential to further damage his candidacy.

But King didn't light the blowtorch. Perhaps he was happy that Cam had answered his demand to call in and instead of raising policy issues he questioned the candidate in general terms about the McEwen electorate and the upcoming poll. It was a much-needed win for Cameron.

Cam campaigned incessantly in the final week of the campaign and with the general polls tightening many believed there was still a chance he could win. Tremors were going through the Labor Party because it was becoming clear they could be chucked out of office in an eventuality that would render the Gillard putsch to oust Rudd one of the great debacles of Australian political history.

On election day Cam told the media at Diamond Creek that he was hopeful the Liberals would hold on to the seat but as he travelled west into the new housing areas the response from locals was less than encouraging. A significant number of people just ignored him. They looked straight through him. Nevertheless, preparations were underway for a night of celebrations at the Kinglake pavilion. Food had been ordered, one of the KFNC committeemen had stocked the bar and the TV crews began to roll up midafternoon.

By 5.30 P.M., with only half an hour to go until the polls closed, Tony Gibbs the barman was there along with all the TV people and print media but there were no locals.

An hour later there were still only a handful of locals, including Mark Beacham and one of his helpers. Cam had some stiff competition for a crowd. An ABBA cover group was playing locally, there was also a twenty-first birthday and the footballers had stayed home because they had a big final to play the following day.

Cam, Laura and the boys arrived before 7 P.M. as the first results began to come through. Shortly afterwards McEwen flashed up on the TV screen and initially it showed Cam and Mitchell running neck and neck with barely 2% of votes counted.

However, within half an hour it was obvious that the anti-Labor swing sweeping through the northern states petered out at the Victorian border. People south of the Murray River were sticking with Gillard, or at least refusing to transfer their allegiance to Abbott.

McEwen updates then showed, as expected, the Greens polling over 11% and with at least three out of four of their preferences flowing to Labor, Cam was going to need a big primary vote lead if he was to have any chance of victory.

It never eventuated; in fact Mitchell led slightly on primary votes and with the Meacher Green preferences thrown in it was clear as early as 8 P.M. that it was all over. There was a subdued atmosphere at the clubrooms as workers filtered back in from the polling booths.

In Victoria the Liberals were hard pressed to hold a number of seats. Cam thanked his supporters and refused to concede victory to Mitchell, but in the deeper recesses of his mind he was already back in a blue police uniform.

There was also a nagging sense of relief. He knew he was capable of carrying the good fight to Canberra on behalf of local people but he wasn't sure he was ready for the arcane world of professional politics or the cut and thrust of the Westminster parliamentary system. In fact, he didn't even know how that system worked.

After five weeks of hard campaigning he was no more comfortable in a politician's skin than when the electioneering had started.

Two days later he applied to rejoin the Victoria Police. However, it took six weeks for the force to accept him back. Cam suspected some people may have been deliberately putting the "slows" on his return to the ranks and he was forced to work with a mate on plumbing jobs just to make ends meet.

Eventually, in the second week of October, he was back on the Kinglake beat. Coincidently his partner on his first shift was Roger Wood. They hadn't worked together since February 7, 2009.

The 2010 federal election result was so close it was weeks before Julia Gillard was able to form a new Labor Government, and she could only do it with the help of independent MPs. History will show that it was always unlikely Cameron Caine would hold the seat of McEwen for the Liberals, but if he had succeeded against the odds, as he did during Black Saturday, Gillard would probably not have been able to form a government.

A couple of weeks after he was back on the beat Cam got a call from 104 that stopped him in his tracks. With the Victorian state election looming on the horizon Mike Laker had pulled out of the contest. Laker had been on the losing end of a racial row and was adamant he'd been "done over" by Labor.

It was a potentially crucial decision because, in an action replay of the federal election, the polls had begun to tighten and it looked like the Brumby Labor Government would be counting on Green preferences to scrape back into office.

Tony Nutt wanted to know if Cam would consider standing for the seat of Seymour! The senior constable smiled to himself. He had believed all along that he was more suited to state politics, with its emphasis on everyday issues, than the top-heavy policy items that would have been on his agenda in Canberra.

But Cam also knew that the sitting member, Labor's Ben Hardman, had strong support and a comfortable 7% electoral cushion. Plus it wouldn't be fair on Laura and the family for him to stand again so soon after they had devoted everything to the federal campaign. He declined Nutt's offer.

The Liberals turned to business consultant Cindy McLeish as their candidate. On the morning of the election two opinion polls showed that after eleven years in government, Labor could be facing defeat in Victoria, and indeed that was the way it played out.

Hardman was put to the sword with an 11.3% swing against him. McLeish, the new kid in town, also suffered a 2.4% swing against her on the primary vote. But once the preferences kicked in it was clear McLeish had the support of a sizeable group of people who were vehemently opposed to that North-South pipeline which took water from the Goulburn River and sent it to Melbourne.

McLeish won the seat by more than 1,200 votes and helped the Liberals form a coalition government with a two-seat majority.

Ted Baillieu was to be the new premier. Cameron could only shake his head and smile.

Cam and Ross take some time out. (Pic: family collection.)

CHAPTER 6

FINALE

THE WEEK AFTER Cam's political career came to an end Ross was up on stage at the Tin Shed, a small auditorium with a concrete floor at Kinglake's Community Village, where bushfire victims lived in portable two-bedroom units.

More than 120 people were crowded inside. Black plastic was draped over the windows to darken the room and a huge goldmining backdrop was lit up on the stage. There was a sense of expectation that something special was about to happen.

Actors wearing nineteenth century police costumes collected "mining licences", which doubled as admission tickets. Staff in period costume were handing out elaborate programs which contained song lyrics and the history of goldmining in the region while others were preparing damper and strawberry jam treats.

Pay Dirt – The Musical! was coming alive after weeks of hard work by Ross, Bec and a small army of Kinglakers.

The pre-show set-up was extraordinarily professional but could the show itself live up to expectations or would it just be a bunch of amateurs relying on the goodwill of the audience to get through the next seventy minutes?

Local politicians, including federal MP elect Rob Mitchell, were among the audience as well as media and a sprinkling of visitors from out of town.

Wally Spezza and Aiden Buchanan were up on stage in the band section while Bec, the stage manager, was running some last-minute checks. Ross stood with a guitar slung around his neck waiting patiently for her signal. Bec dimmed the lights and on cue Ross welcomed people to a matinee performance of his play.

He looked very focused, verging on nervous, but it became clear as the rollicking band launched into its first song that he was in the zone. Zen Buddhists call it "objectless awareness", Ross seemed aware of nothing beyond the song he played, beyond the moment.

Like a proud father, he skilfully guided the band, the players and the audience through his creation.

Pay Dirt – The Musical is a quirky and colourful story set in Kinglake and neighbouring St Andrews during the 1880s and includes a token Indigenous character, called Token, an oppressed Chinese miner, some oppressive troopers, an American immigrant and the miner Dale and his wife Grace.

Grace's role in the play is dedicated to Neeve Grace Buchanan.

Ross had cleverly woven VBRRA into the script in the guise of a mining authority; in fact, his anti-authoritarian streak permeated the play.

Of course there was lots of goodwill in the audience, people wanted to see the play succeed because Ross, Bec and the others had put so much work into it. But after a few minutes the goodwill was superfluous, it was apparent the play was standing up on its own merits. Soon enough people were laughing and applauding spontaneously.

At the interval the audience tucked into the damper and strawberry jam and enthused how surprisingly slick and professional the production was considering it had been put together by a bunch of local Kinglakers.

The second half of the play proved even more engaging than the first with plenty of laughs, some affecting moments and jaunty songs that were quick to have people bouncing around in their seats. As the play progressed it was clear that goldmining was just the bedrock upon which other themes of racism and "have a go" were constructed. Ross's friends would have been surprised if *Pay Dirt* didn't have a sharp cutting edge.

Fittingly the play climaxed with one of Neeve's favourite songs, "In the Land Downunder", which has a catchy foot-stompin' and hand-clappin' chorus –

Congratulations

You multi cultured nation

Without you we'd be lost,

Like havin' no Southern Cross

We're all grateful that you're here

It don't matter where ya from

When ya singin this song

It's a mad mad world

No worries in the land Downunder

(Have a Go)

As the chorus was reprised some members of the audience climbed up on the stage and joined in, while others leapt to their feet clapping their hands. Again and again they sang the chorus. It was as if they didn't want the moment to end.

A warm and rich feeling of bonhomie swept through the shed, people seemed to be aware they were taking part in an extraordinary event. Importantly, it was something beyond the fires, something with only a passing reference to bushfire recovery.

It gave a glimpse of a possible new life for Ross, particularly if he and the crew could find enough money to take *Pay Dirt* on the road and perform at schools and halls around the state.

As had been the case with the Thank You Melbourne concert it was a triumph. It was a momentous achievement for the Kinglake community to produce Thank You Melbourne and *Pay Dirt* out of the Black Saturday ashes. Both productions enjoyed success in no small part because of the Buchanan ying and yang, Ross's creativity and Bec's organisational skills.

Ross enjoys a beer after the Pay Dirt – The Musical *matinee. Wally is in front of him and Aiden is in the background enjoying a cold Coke. (Pic: family collection.)*

Among the audience on that Sunday afternoon in Kinglake was a local state MP Donna Petrovich. She spoke about *Pay Dirt* in the Victorian Parliament.

"This clever musical showcased the talents of musicians, actors and those who baked and served the scones and damper. All are residents of the Kinglake Ranges.

"The great pity is that unless funding can be sourced this musical will not bring pleasure to other communities, in particular those which are bushfire affected.

"I know there is a great desire by those who have put the show together to tour some of the larger regional centres but in particular those still-struggling fire-affected communities which could do with a laugh and the enjoyment that this play would bring both young and old.

"I keep hearing that these communities would like a hand up and not a handout. It's a shame that with so much money being wasted in red tape that suitable funding could not be provided to ensure that this Victorian-produced show could not be a showcase of what can be achieved.

"I would love to see this troupe on the road and showing the people of Victoria what a talented community exists at Kinglake. Lots of fun, a little bit of history and great bush band music. Very Australian and more people deserve the opportunity to see *Pay Dirt – The Musical*."

A week after Donna Petrovich spoke there was no sign of any support and, worse, no sign of anyone taking an interest in *Pay Dirt*. Bec was paying more than $2,000 a month to lease that big goldmining backdrop. The Buchanans were running short of money. Ross had a frightening thought, what if all the months of hard work he had put into the play amounted to nothing and the only place the musical stayed alive was in "Google land"?

In desperation he prepared to fire off a vitriolic email slamming politicians, VBRRA and various others he bore grudges against because they had failed to support *Pay Dirt*. He pointed out it was one of the few good and original ideas to come out of Kinglake since the fires. It also potentially provided meaningful employment for local people.

For good measure he included other complaints in the email, such as the shire's failure to clear a fallen tree from Mick and Jenny's garage. His parents-in-law dubbed him the keyboard warrior. Eventually he agreed to take some of the sting out of the rhetoric before sending the email, but it was still so strident it elicited an immediate response from the shire about removing the tree and zero response from everyone else.

Much of Ross's world was destroyed by fire in 2009 and two years later he was burning his bridges and feeling increasingly isolated and frustrated. Day after day he felt so angry he could explode. He felt as if he could stand in the backyard facing the blackened trees and hurl what was left of his heart into the forest.

It was time to call Cameron.

Suggested Referrals for Those Seeking Assistance

1. Speak to your GP (they can talk to you about options for receiving therapeutic assistance)
2. Contact Beyond Blue Info Line – 1300 22 4636
3. Contact Lifeline – 13 11 14
4. Contact Australian Psychological Society – 1800 333 497

Ross and Cameron

RAW THOUGHTS

Cameron Where Have Those Two Years Gone?

CAMERON PENNED THESE thoughts on the second anniversary of Black Saturday.

As we approach the second anniversary of Black Saturday I sit and wonder, "Where have those two years gone?" Although the time has flown by, I can remember the 7th of February 2009 as if it was yesterday.

It was only last night I watched a re-run of the documentary *Inside the Firestorm*. I was once again paralysed by the visions and the interviews. As Ross's father-in-law Mick Clark relived his night of the fires he said that three police vehicles turned up to help get his wife Jenny to the hospital, my eyes welled up. A lump the size of a football grew in my chest. Mick repeated twice, "These guys were a godsend." I broke down again.

Over the past two years I have been nominated for the Australian of the Year "Local Hero" award, been one of the *Herald Sun*'s top 10 inspirational people of 2009, I have been honoured to receive the Victoria Police Valour Award and have been informed I am to receive the Australasian Humanitarian Silver Medal. I have been the Liberal candidate for McEwen, where I rubbed shoulders with the leaders of our great country, and I was privileged to play a role on the biggest day on the Australian sporting calendar when I carried the AFL cup onto the MCG on Grand Final day in 2009. The list goes on.

It goes without saying I would hand it all back tomorrow if just one of my friends could return to his or her pre-Black Saturday life.

I have made some fantastic new friends through all these new experiences. I value these friendships dearly. I have learned so much in such a short period of time.

I still find it hard to accept thank-yous for saving people's lives that night. Although it's humbling it makes me uncomfortable. To this day one lasting memory haunts me, and I still tear up in the presence of Ross "Rossi" Laudisio.

I cherished those late-night coffees at Cappa Rossi's restaurant, sitting around the table with Rossi, his sister Isabella and father "Papa", sorting out the world and talking about our little quiet part of the universe, Kinglake. So much had happened in such a short time when I came across Rossi that night. From the loss of his father to then locating his wife and children who he mistakenly thought had also perished. Then afterwards driving to Kinglake and being present with Roger when he informed Isabella of the passing of her father. This is one of the most memorable moments for me.

There was so much emotion in such a short time. Memories flood back on anniversaries and at ceremonies. They flood back on hot windy days, and sometimes just lying in bed, but I value what I have now more than I ever did before February 7, 2009.

As I look over my back fence and see the ferns returned and the trees dropping the blackened bark from their vast heights, I look at what needs to be done. There are still fences to be fixed and firewood to be cut, split and stacked. Over the past two years I have neglected the home duties as I have been so busy.

As I look around I ask myself many questions: "Am I happy here in Kinglake, am I still happy working at the Kinglake Police Station, has the community changed?" As I'm turning forty this year I'm calling it my midlife crisis.

The community has changed, and of course it would. My major concern now two years on is that there's a chance our fire-affected community could become a welfare state. This is a harsh statement, I know, but I do not apologise for this. I believe the families of the 173 people who perished on February 7, 2009, should be assisted in any and every way they can. I can't imagine the hurt and the feeling of loss and anger if I had my family taken from me. And no parent should ever have to bury their child, no matter how old. But unfortunately there are some others who refuse to take hold of their own destiny and move on. I know it's hard but I am afraid they will be left behind.

I've returned to my position at the Kinglake Police Station where I love going to work with some terrific guys. When Roger came back to work at the station, ironically, our first shift together was exactly 20 months to the day of Black Saturday. Even in the weeks after the fires Roger and I did not work together.

I often sit behind my desk and think there is more to life than being here as a senior constable at Kinglake. In the past two years I have seen and done so much. What does the future hold? I don't know. I have learned to say "never say never"!

To my family, Laura, Sian, Angus and Harry, I worship the ground you guys walk on. I now get up every morning and think how lucky I am. I thank you for your love and support over the past two years and thank you for being there with me and for me.

To my mum and dad, I thank you for being there for my whole family and for your support over the past two years in all my journeys, both good and bad.

To Ross and Bec, I have learned so much from you both, your strength is amazing. Ross, I value our road trips to do our talks and I still stand there amazed at your strength and your good heartedness and your desire to help the teenage kids and the encouragement you give them in whatever they do. Good on ya, bloke!

In finishing, I suppose I can answer the question I have been asking myself for the past eighteen months – "Have I changed?" Whether it's good or bad, I have – the night of February 7, 2009, changed my life forever.

Ross's Response to the Bushfires Royal Commission

Ross sent and received a great deal of correspondence in the ten months after the fires. Some of it, relating to "appropriate payments for the deceased", has already been included.

Ross penned these points after the interim report of the Bushfires Royal Commission was released. He felt that the report implied that he was partly responsible for the deaths of his children because his fire plan was inadequate. These are Ross's sentiments –

1. Our family **successfully** activated our fire plan in the January 2006 fires in the Kinglake Ranges.
2. Despite all those who died or were affected by Ash Wednesday or Canberra fires it sometimes seems we know very little about bushfires and recovery. Maybe this time we'll learn.
3. Our last update was of the imminent threat to Whittlesea (not Kinglake 40kms away)!! By 5.30 pm there was no warning from anyone including our supposed safety nets- radio , our community fire guard, and internet updates which we relied on and expected to receive.
4. Where my 2 children, brother in law and 2 young girls died was classed as the safest house in the street by paid CFA experts.
5. More brick, mud brick and bluestone houses burnt to the ground than other dwellings.
6. The communication system was a failure for our volunteer emergency service workers threatening their lives.

7. Royal Commission Fact, warnings to Kinglake Ranges were issued after the fire front had been through and killed even though warnings could have been issued hours earlier.

8. Emergency assembly points were discontinued by our Shire for fear of repercussions/liability.

Conclusion – Yes Feb 7 turned out to be a devastating day, however we personally felt, as did so many others, that our already successful fire plan, 21st century communications and learning from past mistakes would protect us. We were wrong.

Sincerely yours, an expert at burying loved ones way before their time.

Have We Learned?

This letter was sent to Ross (as well as politicians and officials) by a survivor of the 2003 Canberra bushfires. Ross feels the author, a member of The Singed Sisterhood (see below), has an accurate and comprehensive understanding of what the Black Saturday survivors are going through. The letter has undergone minor editing.

As I sit watching TV news coverage, with my heart racing and my body shaking slightly as I remember the fear, the flames, the heat, the smoke and the knowledge that I would probably not get out alive, I also remember in the days, weeks and months after the fires what support we needed and valued.

The victims of the Victorian fires are coping with the loss of homes, possessions, pets and property as well as trying to cope with immense grief.

A great relief effort is one that is based on the experiences of previous disaster situations, and yet, after the Canberra bushfires, we were so often "re-inventing the wheel".

I just can't bear to see those victims in Victoria not benefit from what we learned in Canberra.

While the aid agencies will swing into action, and do what they do best, and the state and federal governments put their disaster planning into action, how can the Australian public, and the Victorian Relief Effort, help in the best way possible?

What the surviving victims need, both in terms of donations and physical and emotional support, will come in phases. Of course, the first weeks after the fire, in the immediate post trauma phase, these needs will be different from what they will need in six, twelve months' or two years' time.

So, for what it's worth, here are my tips for a "great" relief.

Notes to the General Public

Donate cash. Every little bit counts. If every person in Australia donated just five dollars, imagine what a difference it would make.

Basic essentials. Please only donate things that are new or of good quality.

Think of all the things you need every day: pyjamas, toothbrush, toothpaste, face washer, soap, toiletries bag, deodorant, hairbrush, comb, shampoo, clothes suitable for work, casual clothes, belt, shoes, socks, watch, hair ties, wallet, handbag, keyring, hat, sunscreen etc. These people have nothing. While they will receive immediate assistance in the form of cash and gift vouchers from charitable organisations for major retail outlets, I remember that every day there was something I needed and didn't have. Within the first few days we needed notepads and pens just to deal with the paperwork and the insurance company.

Needs change over time, as people move into temporary accommodation they will need cooking utensils, pots, pans, plates, cups, bowls, kitchen knives, furniture, TVs, beds… the list is endless.

Cold weather will come in another month or two and winter clothes will be needed at this time – warm tops, coats, hats and scarves. Blankets, electric blankets and heaters will also be needed. I distinctly remember the day the weather suddenly turned cold in Canberra and no one in the family had a warm top to wear.

Make something. Some of our most treasured items are the ones that were made, with love, by complete strangers. The quilt that was one of the hundreds that arrived from all over Australia, the hand-knitted rugs that my children like to snuggle under in winter. If you make jewellery, make a few pairs of earrings or a necklace. If you make toys, make something for the children who have lost theirs. If you knit, make a winter scarf. If you sew, make some table placemats or a beautiful table runner. If you're an artist, paint a picture or frame a drawing.

I still find it incredibly moving that people cared enough to put time and love into making something that has now become a new family treasure for us.

Grow something. Those that remain, and those that decide to rebuild, face a blackened, denuded landscape. If you live within reasonable distance of the bushfire area, pot some seedlings and start growing some vegetation to help rejuvenate the gardens that were lost. Contact your local nursery, land care or conservation group to see what vegetation is drought resistant and/or native to the area. In Canberra, a very successful Garden Regeneration Scheme was set up by volunteers and in the two-year period after the fires, they helped many, many people re-landscape their gardens. To see green, to see new growth, when we returned to our rebuilt home, was not only beautiful but gave us hope that we too could recover.

Kids. My three children were young at the time of the fires, so I remember well how grateful I was when we received toys, colouring-in books, pencils and textas, craft items, DVDs, books to read and pushbikes.

Friends and acquaintances. If you personally know someone who was affected, every little gesture of help and support helps. Bake some biscuits or a meal and drop it around to them, offer to put their washing on the line, offer to do their supermarket shopping, offer to mind their kids. I remember feeling so overwhelmed and so busy answering phone calls and organising basic survival that I simply didn't have time or energy to cook meals, wash, clean and do all the other things that keep a family going – this went on for months.

This help will be invaluable in coming weeks and months.

Notes to Victorian Disaster Relief Organisers

Counselling: Don't sit the counsellors in a room at the recovery centres where people have to go to them. These victims are in shock and running on adrenaline. The women will usually talk about it, the men won't. Men seldom seek out emotional assistance or counselling. Often the men will hold it all inside and release it in anger or violence a few days, weeks, months or years down the track. Years on from the fires, women were saying that their husbands "didn't talk about it" and were withdrawn or showing signs of depression.

Put the counsellors and social workers in the field. Get them to go and help the men sort through the burnt out remainders of their homes. Get them to go to the pubs and clubs where the men are congregating. Get them to be there when the bulldozers move in to flatten what little remains of people's homes. Often people just want someone to listen and to tell them that what they are experiencing is "normal" under the circumstances.

Get the social workers to be there to act as advocates when victims have to deal with public servants, banks, and government officials in the next few weeks. Some of the victims will have literally lost their identities – they will have no wallet, no identification, no bank details. They will have to deal with insurance companies and government agencies. People working in these institutions don't have training as social workers, and often are under increased stress themselves. I can't tell you the number of victims who were coping pretty well up until they had to deal with a bank or other institution who were either obstructive or unable to assist because "our computer system won't let me".

Buddy system: Our children's school instituted a "buddy system" for the families from school that lost their homes. This was a fantastic system that could be adapted for use in any disaster situation. Hundreds of people were phoning, dropping into our temporary accommodation and offering help, but it was so overwhelming. People kept asking "What do you need" and it was very hard to say "Everything." Our buddy removed this stress so that when people asked "What do you need?" or "What can I do?" we referred them to our buddy.

Women's networks: As well as dealing with trauma, pain and grief, women have to look after the needs of their family. This can mean they put their own needs last.

My greatest source of support and friendship was a small group of women bound by the fact that our children all attended the same school and we all lost our homes. We started meeting for coffee a few weeks after the fires and, six years on, we still meet regularly for lunch. We call ourselves The Singed (as in "slightly burnt") Sisterhood.

I don't know how I would have got through the last six years without these wonderful women who have now become close friends.

Communication: The victims of the fires will be spreading across the state, and in some cases interstate, to stay with relatives and friends. It is vital that all victims stay connected to the network of aid that will be coming their way in the following weeks, months and years.

While I know a database of victims is currently being compiled, it is imperative that this database is updated as victims move from temporary accommodation into rental accommodation and then decide to rebuild, buy or rent indefinitely.

Often, those that had immediate help, staying in fully furnished homes, or with friends or family for extended periods, miss out on some assistance in the immediate phase because they don't need it, however this puts them at a disadvantage further down the track in a few months' time, when this accommodation ceases and they then have to begin again with nothing. The aid will need to be ongoing.

Not everyone will have access to a computer, certainly not in the first few weeks, or even months. Post information to people – mail can be forwarded or passed on.

Shopping centres: Everyone needs to shop – particularly if you've lost everything. Distribute newsletters updating victims and survivors on what is happening and what help they can access via shopping centres around the state. Libraries, government offices, community centres, cultural and religious centres can also distribute the newsletters.

These newsletters can also inform members of the public how they can help.

Mobile phone bills: Most of us faced enormous mobile phone bills after the fires. In the weeks and months after the fires, our mobiles were our lifeline – to friends, family, work, the insurance company, to everything. In the weeks after the fires, I used my mobile more than I ever have in my life. In the months after the fires, when we were already under huge stress, we had to pay huge mobile phone bills.

At the time of the Canberra fires, I was not aware of any mobile phone providers who took this into consideration by negating or reducing mobile phone bills for victims (I would love to be proved wrong on this).

Survivors: Consider the survivors who did not lose their homes so have to return to a devastated community. Please don't keep saying to them "Well, at least you didn't lose your house." They are going through such mixed emotions after losing friends and neighbours that they may have mixed emotions about being "spared."

They have to return to the devastated landscape and try and rebuild their lives. Their children will play in ash and dirt, the amount of dust and debris flying through the air is unbelievable. They will spend the next year or so cleaning constantly and yet everything will still remain covered in a layer of fine ash and dust. They won't be able to hang clothes on the line because they come in dirtier than when they went out. These seem like insignificant things, but when these things happen after a tragedy such as this, when you've lost friends and neighbours, and your support networks have gone, they make a very traumatic situation even more stressful.

Note to the Victims

Learn to receive: Most of us are great at giving help, but many people find it difficult to accept help. Take the help when it is offered and don't be afraid to ask for what you need. For many people it can be incredibly hard to do this. While at the moment you have no choice but to accept help, it may be hard to keep accepting help months and years down the track. But you need to allow family, friends, and the wider community to give. It will make you stronger and, years from now, will be an incredible insight into what others need in times of trauma – because you've been there and you understand. The only way you can truly learn to help others is by accepting help yourself when you need it.

www.ingramcontent.com/pod-product-compliance
Lightning Source LLC
Chambersburg PA
CBHW020520080526
44583CB00013B/673